"Each of us finds a comfortable position somewhere along the continuum that ranges from complete withdrawal and self-absorption at one end to full civic engagement and reciprocity at the other. The position is never fixed. We fret, vacillate and steer our lives through the riptide of countervailing instincts that press from both ends of the continuum. The uncertainty we feel is not a curse. It is not a confusion on the road out of Eden. It is just the human condition. We are intelligent mammals, fitted by evolution—by God, if you prefer—to pursue personal ends through cooperation..."

– Edward O. Wilson
The Future of Life

THE CREATIVE COMMUNITY

Designing for Life

"A day spent without the sight or sound of beauty, the contemplation of mystery, or the search for truth and perfection is a poverty-stricken day; and a succession of such days is fatal to human life."

– Lewis Mumford

Vernon D. Swaback, FAIA, FAICP

"The individual, if left alone from birth, would remain primitive and beastlike in his thoughts and feelings to a degree that we can hardly conceive. The individual is what he is and has the significance that he has not so much in virtue of this individuality, but rather as a member of a great human community, which directs his material and spiritual existence from the cradle to the grave."

– Albert Einstein

First published in Australia in 2003 by
The Images Publishing Group Pty Ltd.
ABN 89 059 734 431
6 Bastow Place, Mulgrave, Victoria 3170, Australia
Telephone +613 9561 5544 Facsimile +613 9561 4860
Email: books@images.com.au
www.imagespublishing.com.au

Printing rights: Copyright © The Images Publishing Group Pty Ltd. 2003
Contents: Copyright © 2003 Vernon D. Swaback, FAIA, FAICP
7550 East McDonald Drive
Scottsdale, AZ 85250, USA
Telephone: (480) 367-2100
Facsimile: (480) 367-2101
Email: vswaback@swabackpartners.com

The Images Publishing Group Reference Number: 507

ISBN 1 920744 15 0

Edited by Karen Werner
Research Assistant: Sarah Hankins

Designed by Studio V Graphics of Swaback Partners
Production by The Graphic Image Studio Pty Ltd. Melbourne, Australia

Film by Mission Productions Limited
Printed by Sing Cheong Printing Co. Ltd. Hong Kong

Cover: The Village of Kohler, Wisconsin
as presented in Chapter Nine

End papers: Studies for DC Ranch, Scottsdale, Arizona
as presented in Chapter Eight

Dedicated to all

who harbor visions

of a better world

while working

to make incremental

improvements

in the here and now.

"As you enter positions of trust and power,
dream a little before you think."

– Toni Morrison

Contents

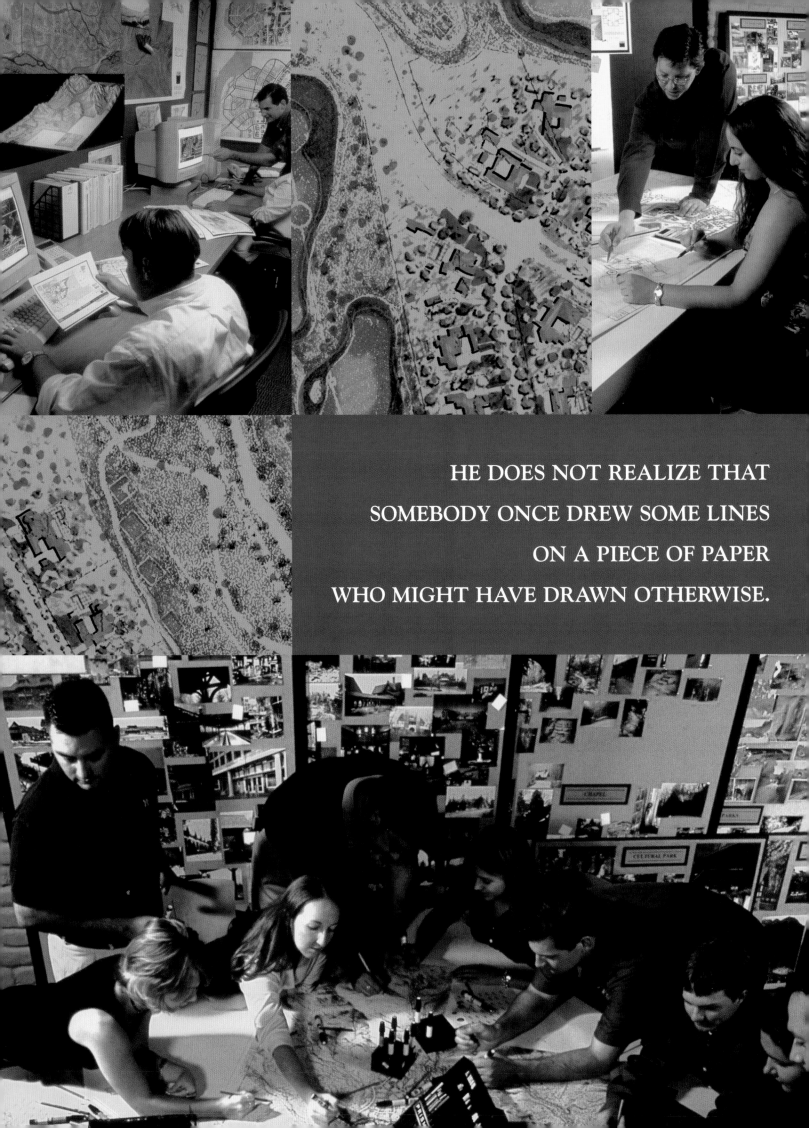

HE DOES NOT REALIZE THAT
SOMEBODY ONCE DREW SOME LINES
ON A PIECE OF PAPER
WHO MIGHT HAVE DRAWN OTHERWISE.

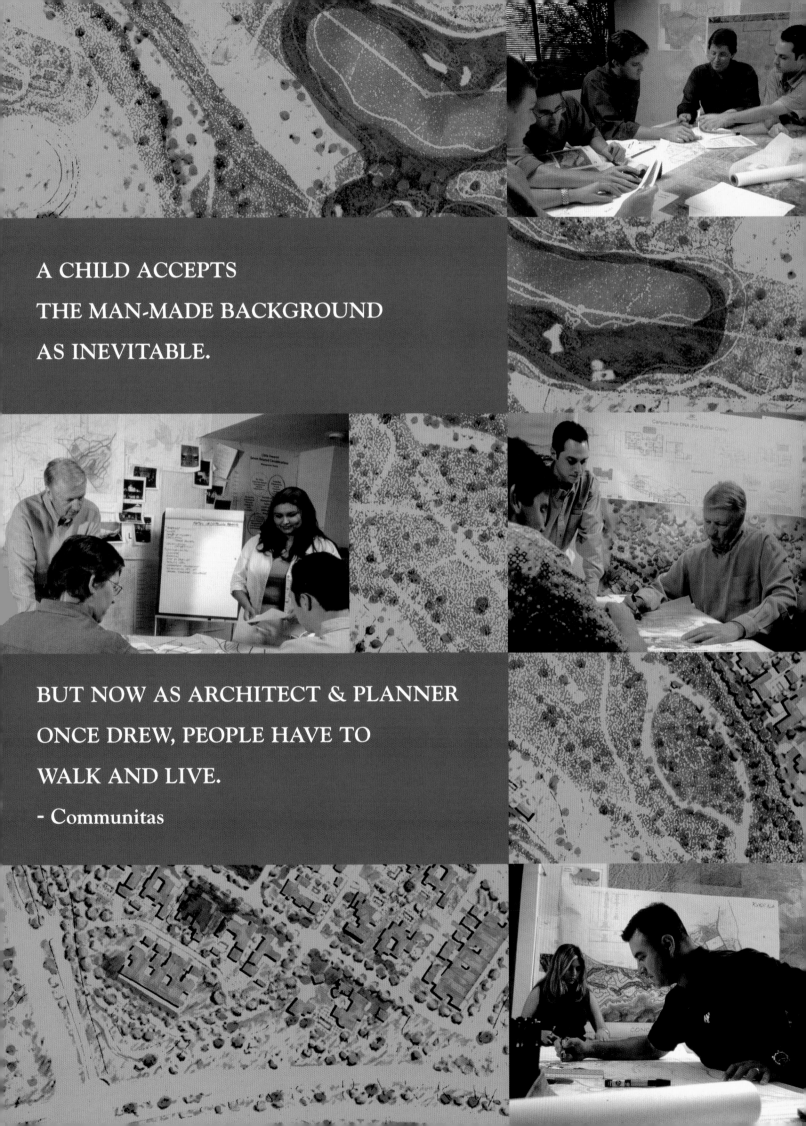

A CHILD ACCEPTS
THE MAN-MADE BACKGROUND
AS INEVITABLE.

BUT NOW AS ARCHITECT & PLANNER
ONCE DREW, PEOPLE HAVE TO
WALK AND LIVE.

- Communitas

About the Chapter Pages

Claude Monet, one of the world's most celebrated Impressionist painters, considered the garden he created in Giverny, just north of Paris, to be his greatest work of art. Views into his garden appear at the beginning of each chapter to symbolize the power of creativity and stewardship.

While Monet had to request permission from local authorities to expand his garden, no amount of codes, ordinances or jurisdictional review could ever bring about such beauty. And while the garden was a personal pursuit, the magnetism of what Monet created on just five acres continues to attract and inspire a half million people each year who come from all over the world to see his living legacy. In keeping with the thesis of this book, Monet's creation of this special environment was inseparable from the vitality of his 86 years of life and work.

Some years ago, while judging an urban design studio at a leading university, I used the word "beauty." The professor who was observing the judging said, "Beauty—now that's a word we don't hear much around here." I remember thinking that the entries in the competition made it painfully clear that there were other words that had fallen into disuse, like authenticity, grace, charm and character. These are all words of individuality that suffer in public debate, because they have no easy measure. Monet's garden serves to remind us that things that are truly worthwhile, like care, love and nurture, exist in a realm far beyond that which can be legislated or enforced, and certainly beyond anything that can be argued into existence.

Community as Performance

There has long been a philosophical connection between architecture and music. Frank Lloyd Wright said he learned to see architecture as an edifice of sound. Goethe described architecture as frozen music. Carrying the analogy further, if the custom house is equivalent to a solo, and the greater metropolitan area a symphony, the creative community is equivalent to a chamber ensemble. Every musician knows that in a chamber ensemble each member must perform as a leader and as part of the group. Because of this dual role, the chamber ensemble is regarded to be the highest form of music making.

The commitment and awareness of each participant heightens the energy and performance of the others. In like manner, the creative community is the highest form of human settlement, because a shared commitment to human values enriches both the individual and the group. What we have yet to learn is that, like music, the creative community can be "performed" at ever higher levels of skill and satisfaction. The first step toward creating more than what already exists is to get past the confusing preconceptions that limit our notion of the possible. Beyond such self-defeating barriers exists an endless variety of ways to design environments that provide a more rewarding balance between the desire for privacy and the connectedness and stimulation that is possible only by way of community.

Foreword

William H. Hudnut III

William Hudnut holds the Urban Land Foundation/Joseph C. Canizaro Chair for Public Policy at the Urban Land Institute, a nonprofit organization dedicated to providing responsible leadership in the use of land. He is a former congressman and four-term mayor of Indianapolis, where he spearheaded the formation of a public/private partnership that led to Indianapolis's emergence as an entrepreneurial American city. William Hudnut served as past president of the National League of Cities and the Indiana Association of Cities and is the recipient of 12 honorary degrees; Princeton University's highest alumni honor, the Woodrow Wilson Award for public service; the Rosa Parks Award from the American Association for Affirmative Action; the Gibson Award from the Indiana American Institute of Architects; and the Distinguished Public Service Award from the Indiana Association of Cities and Towns. During his tenure in office he was named by City and State *magazine as the "Nation's Best Mayor."*

A key question America will be facing in the next 20 years is: how will we grow as a nation? There will be 60 million more people in the United States in 2020 than there were at the turn of the century. They will have to live somewhere. Many will want to live in the suburbs, even though the typical "Ozzie and Harriet" family household no longer constitutes even one-quarter of the population. Some cohorts—generation X and Yers and aging baby boomers—may have grown tired of suburban living and desire the amenities of an urban lifestyle. Latinos, a growing segment of our population, will want single-family housing. Fourteen percent of our working families have critical housing needs, defined as either living in severely substandard housing or spending 30–50 percent of their income on housing.

Both as designer and author, Vernon Swaback has long been on a mission to lift our insights above the kinds of self-defeating arguments that can so easily dominate public testimony. His integrated approach to architecture and planning has been uncommonly successful in gaining approvals for the design of projects involving major changes to the status quo. He and his colleagues are crusaders for land-use decisions to be guided by human values and the pursuit of community, rather than allowing prevailing prejudices or the easier-to-measure dictates of codes and ordinances to shape what we build.

Swaback is not alone in such crusading, but an increasing array of books and articles inflict harsh judgments on so-called suburban sprawl, only to offer slight changes or no new vision at all. What makes this book remarkable is its clarity concerning why we have so much of what we say we don't want.

Growth is inevitable, driving economic progress. The issue is whether or not it necessitates the continuing development of new land. Swaback appeals for a new ethic of land use and development. He wants readers to appreciate a new paradigm for land-use professionals that emphasizes better quality rather than simply more quantity. No development is better than poor development. Understanding that issuing a series of permits that consumes land but does not add up to a city, only one new subdivision, one new shopping center, one new office park at a time, he asks, "Must our codes and ordinances not only preclude the worst but also the best?" He asserts that "to build with boldness and sensitivity is to add to the beauty of the land," and queries, "Why not a 'Variance for Excellence' so that human integration might join forces with nature, as has often happened in the past?"

Many Americans have tired of sprawling development and its unintended consequences: traffic congestion and long commutes, the cost of new infrastructure, environmental degradation, loss of greenspace, and the disappearing sense of community. They long for a sense of place. They want a feeling of belonging, of roots and centeredness. They still like single-family housing but are discontent with the rest of the suburban package, the patchwork of strip centers and asphalt parking lots, single-use zoning that creates separate pods of retail, residential and office development, mind-numbing monotony, unattractive design and automobile dependence. Eleven different studies have shown that given the choice between compact centers and commercial strips, consumers prefer the centers by a wide margin. They like public spaces such as plazas, cafés, taverns, town squares, village greens, parks, amphitheaters, sidewalks, walkable streets, pathways and greenways. Around the country, we are seeing some 100 new town-center projects and more than 6000 renovations of main streets, answering the consumer demand for urban-scale, mixed-use developments in suburban settings.

In this new book, Swaback addresses these issues with beautiful language and imagery. He put his dream of artful design into words and pictures that should lift the spirits of all his readers. He has labored for four decades in the heat of the day, battling fear and prejudice, holding all comers to a high standard. So it is not as though he were sitting in an ivory tower conjuring up a fantasyland for the built environment. He knows where the rubber hits the road, and he knows—indeed, believes with all his heart and soul and mind—that we can do better in the future than we have in the near past. He has the courage to join forces against the de-densifying, centrifugal tendencies of promiscuous land consumption, boldly asserting that "the artless fragmentation of the past was easier," and warning us that "if we want to keep doing exactly as we have in the past, we will get the same results in the future. This limited view," he adds, "is a self-fulfilling trap."

Swaback understands why we have tended to favor privacy over community, reminding us that the "sovereignty of the individual" is a cornerstone of our national heritage. He seeks a balance between our desire for privacy and the rewards of community, especially the kind of community that can enhance experiences at all ages and stages of life.

To point us toward different, more positive and artful results, Swaback takes us on a poetic journey from Camden, Maine to Celebration, Florida, from Central Park to the desert, from Kohler, Wisconsin to Charleston, South Carolina, from tiny Northampton, Massachusetts to the 8,300-acre DC Ranch in Scottsdale, Arizona, from the work of Frederick Law Olmsted to that of his mentor and friend, Frank Lloyd Wright. Indeed, he even takes us overseas to Venice. Constantly, he reminds us of the importance of design in enriching our daily lives and nurturing "personal pride and a shared sense of belonging." We learn how beautifully landscaped parks, restored historic buildings, rezoned streets, public art and public spaces, revitalized waterfronts, transit stops, "lovingly designed structures," the creative use of color and light, and harmonizing with the land and nature can add value to the built environment.

Swaback's themes of "regenerative value" and "retrofitting suburbia" put us in touch with something that will become more prominent in what some are calling the "re-century" that we have only recently entered. Reconstruction, rehabilitation, redesign, refining, rebuilding, re-urbanization, and renewal will become a larger part of our land-use world. Not that it will supersede new development, but restorative development will assume higher priority as we seek to preserve our heritage and conserve our environment after the "dys-urbanization" of the last century. As Swaback so aptly writes, "The future will not only permit but depend on others to re-use, rekindle and in some cases entirely replace what we have done."

Vernon Swaback is "an effective visionary," to borrow his own phrase, opting to be a change agent rather than one who wishes for the future to be more like the past. He wants our communities to be shaped by choice, not chance. We may not agree with every hypothesis he advances, every point he makes, but he certainly stimulates our thinking, addresses key issues of land-use development and community building, generates new ideas and encourages us not to take the path of least resistance.

Taken as a whole, *The Creative Community* is a beautifully hopeful book that will lift our spirits as well as our vision. The German politician Konrad Adenauer once remarked that "we are all born under the same sky, but we don't all have the same horizons." Swaback has a wide horizon, and beckons us to join him in his view. He offers a summons to courageous creativity that will make good things happen in how we live, work and play: "If when we design and develop we are willing to ask ourselves how this will all look and feel 10, 20 and more years from now, we will become more concerned with what matters and less limited by stylistic fashions of the day."

This book is rich in references and imagery of the past, but its focus is squarely on the future. It challenges all of us, no matter what part we may play, to create a better tomorrow by what we design and build today. It is all about bridge-building, between the past and the future, between privacy and community, between what we know and what we do, and between our needs, desires and commitments.

Swaback presents elements of community that are extraordinarily diverse, but they are united by a single idea. In his words, "The most significant communities are not so much the work of specialists as they are the accumulated environments that result from the individual actions of caring people." When he speaks of "designing for life," he is referring to all of us as free-agent shapers of our own houses, neighborhoods, communities and, ultimately, the world.

Because Swaback asks that we consider the built environment as a living laboratory, he uses photographs and captions to describe design principles, rather than offering the more typical information concerning the owners, designers, locations and years of construction. These omissions are not out of neglect but conscious intent. Swaback portrays what he regards to be useful illustrations, no matter what country or which century produced the examples, and why not? Is there any reason why humanity's best cannot be matched or exceeded on our watch? This question is most poignant when addressed to the world's newest and growing settlement patterns, including the suburbs, in which 140,000,000 Americans now live.

As a word of warning, it will be a rare developer who can follow this author without becoming impatient with his many excursions into a deeper sense of purpose. The danger in not doing so is to risk not understanding that it is this more holistic view that is daily reshaping our definition of success.

As is apt for one of Frank Lloyd Wright's last apprentices, Swaback focuses on beauty. But rather than dwelling on style, his emphasis is on the beauty of performance. He insists that when we speak of creating sustainable communities and minimizing the dominance of the automobile, 75 percent of our success toward doing so lies in the realm of human behavior. The best way to influence behavior is by way of designs that inspire us to plan for community at its best.

Whether you simply skim these beautiful pages to renew your excitement for community or intend to read every word, and whether you are a scholar, developer, community leader, planner, architect or what Frank Lloyd Wright called one of our "typical best citizens," this is an amazing work that should be taken to heart. It illuminates a subject that is most often buried in planner's jargon, making it as personal as our own homes, which of course, it is.

Introduction

The success-generating advantages of the creative community are staring us in the face—only our confusion stands in the way. The problem is that our confusion is great. We love low density, but we hate sprawl. We spend billions for public transportation, but more than 90 percent of us don't use it. Our most dominant idea for something "new" is a return to the land-use patterns and circulation systems of the 1920s. We extol the virtues of main street while shopping at Wal-Mart, making it the world's largest employer, not because it generates new wealth but because it cannibalizes the "mom-and-pop" shops of Main Street we say we wish would return. And when we attend seminars to discuss the future, the disconnect between our theology about community and what we actually do is so thorough that to point out the obvious would have a chilling effect on the day.

I was born and raised in the inner city of Chicago, where what the "new urbanists" are now "discovering" had not yet become an innovation—it was too much the norm. I thought all houses had alley-loaded garages, raised front porches and generous walks separated from narrow streets by wide bands of landscaping and a barrier of parked cars. An open, free-flowing grid of streets functioned without freeways, and I don't remember ever seeing a cul-de-sac.

I walked to school, to the park, to my first job, to the dentist, drug store, candy store, and to church, and for recreation, I rode my bicycle. For high school and later college, I road the bus and what we now call light rail. The seasonal changes were very much in evidence, but I don't remember much about the sky.

I left home at 17 to become an apprentice to Frank Lloyd Wright. Winters were spent in the vastness of the mainly empty Sonoran desert, where my exposure to nature, especially the atmospheric effects of the sky, was heightened by living in a tent. Summers were spent in rural south central Wisconsin. For 22 years, at both Taliesin and Taliesin West, I experienced community at a most intensely experimental and cultural level. Following that experience, I started life all over again, living for the first time in an apartment and founding an independent practice of architecture and planning. Now 25 years later, my partners and I have since explored both large and small communities in North and South America, Europe, Japan, Korea, Bhutan, India, Yemen, Tibet, Saudi Arabia and what used to be Yugoslavia, and the far eastern sector of Russia. In our work as architects and planners, we have programmed, planned and designed nearly every variety of structure from custom residences to commercial and institutional buildings. We have planned entire communities, watching over every detail, starting with raw land and continuing through the design of fully operating neighborhoods and town centers.

Anything done well is worthy of admiration. Our regrets are reserved for those thoughtless assumptions that so easily thwart any chance for a higher level of dialogue. Examples include the unexplored but widely held notions about "sprawl" being bad or "light rail" being good. Such oversimplified positions are more about sloganeering than anything to do with achieving a deeper sense of analysis and discovery.

My colleagues and I have been blessed with an extraordinary range of strong and caring clients. We speak not only for ourselves but for them as well in our conviction that community is humanity's most challenging and rewarding achievement. It is challenging because it requires vision, continuity, cooperation between diverse elements, and the need for ongoing renewal. It is rewarding because what we preserve and create today is not only a gift to ourselves, but it is also the greatest gift any one generation can give to the next. The truly creative community is far more than picturesque development. It is the recognition that individual fulfillment is inseparable from the shared quality of life we can only create as a whole.

Clearly, the 21st century is a time of unprecedented opportunity for the development of community, but where do we start? What can we observe about our tendencies and what can we learn from those whose experiences are entirely unlike our own? How willing are we to make long-term commitments and what global changes are in play that will exert influences that we may not yet comprehend? These questions are being addressed in a flood of transformational books with titles like: *The Future of Life*; *Non-Zero: The Logic of Human Destiny*; *The New Geography: How the Digital Revolution Is Reshaping the American Landscape*; *Emergence: The Connected Lives of Ants, Brains, Cities, and Software*; and, *The Rise of the Creative Class and How It's Transforming Work, Leisure, Community, and Everyday Life*.

The Creative Community has been informed by these works and a good many more, but its major insights all come from its author being a participant and sometimes referee on the field of battle—between developers and other agents of change on one side, and those who continue to wish for the future to be more like the past on the other. The "no change" option isn't remotely possible, yet for many, it remains their undying dream. Such views can be quaint but, more often than not, they inflict a loss on the future. This is all about to change, starting with a deeper understanding of how critically important the creation of community is to the success of all other endeavors.

History shows that we live in two worlds: one changes lightning fast, the other glacially slow. Technological advancements in computerization currently dominate the first, while human behavior and the long cool view of nature will always monopolize the second. Since the beginning of time, the record of place-making has been found where these two worlds meet. At the end of the 20th century, the focus of development was largely reduced to the mantras of "location, location, location" and "timing is everything." Location and timing may have been adequate for short-term players to make a financial killing, but they were never adequate for creating community. Wherever special communities exist, they are always the result of uncommon people nurturing uncommon ideas for uncommonly long periods of time. Such places become the "seeing eye" for society. They are heroic, special-case examples that lead to new realities well beyond the formula-driven sterility of suburbia.

While achieving community has never been easy, failure to do so brings with it far greater difficulties and ultimately a threat to our very survival. When the lack of community degenerates to the level of conflict, we look to laws and government to solve the problem. Designers, architects and planners, we think, have a far less serious role to play, all more in the realm of aesthetics. This view is reinforced by efforts that extol the virtues of community in stylistic terms. While "style" has its place, it is not the word one would single out to describe an important work of art. We are on the verge of realizing that there is nothing more creatively significant about that which hangs in a museum than what can and must be expressed in the design of our built environments.

In the region where I make my home, the spread of new development has been clocked at the rate of an acre and a quarter each hour, 24 hours a day, seven days a week. My colleagues and I have presided over precedent-breaking and precedent-setting changes to general plans and zoning. We have led the public sector through successful visioning programs and assisted the private sector in exploring ways to approach development with a broader sense of its ultimate purpose. Because change can seem threatening, we know what it is to feel guilty until proven innocent, and we have experienced the absurdity of lengthy debates resulting in nothing but wasteful exercises, powerless to consider anything worthwhile. Those who shape the built environment, in both the public and private sectors, have never been more weary of giving their all, only to end up with nothing to show for their efforts. We are nearing the point of beneficial change.

This book is the result of four decades of experience on the field of battle. It is a battleground of fears, opinions and prejudices where attacks, influences and support from such a dizzying array of participants can make any hoped-for clarity seem beyond reach.

At the end of such battles, there are always more questions than answers. Will we settle for a future based on the rubble of argument, or are we capable of pursuing communities caressed into being by exploration and design? The answer requires that we examine our conflicting desires between privacy and community, between the past and the future, and between the ease of the expedient and the rewards of a more holistic, long-term vision.

We would all do well to retain the beginner's sense of uncertainty. We would be well served to remain puzzled about the self-defeating ways in which we address our relationships with each other and with the land. The challenge for the 21st century is to view all about us as a living laboratory of cause and effect. A future greater than anything in the past awaits those who see this "living laboratory" as a kind of graduate school in which we are all full-time students.

Vernon D. Swaback, **FAIA, FAICP**
Scottsdale, Arizona

"To whom much is given
much will be required."

—Luke 12:48

"No sooner do you set foot upon American
ground than you are stunned by a kind of tumult.
Everything is in motion..."

—Alexis de Tocqueville, 1835

"America may end in spontaneous combustion,
but never in apathy, inertia or uninventiveness".

—Alistair Cooke, 1952

"In a system in which responsibility is not concentrated
at the center, everyone had better be partly
responsible, so it is for a community,
so it is for a nation — and, most poignantly,
so it is for the only liveable planet we know about."

—John W. Gardner, 1984

Mapping the Journey

One—Examining Our Confusion: If the creation of community were a scientific pursuit, we could simply assign the task to specialists and inhabit the outcome, but that isn't the case. Community is all about human behavior; thus we begin by examining our confusion in order to arrive at a more integrated and powerful way of thinking.

Two—Our Living Laboratory: We easily shrink our view of the possible to what is closest at hand. It is far more empowering to consider the entire earth's experience as rich in lessons for a future both more individually rewarding and collectively beautiful.

Three—American Heritage: What we have created has been inspired from many directions, including our own innovative explorations. From the beginning we have been a nation of dreams. There is much to learn from special places that have been nurtured over time.

Four—Exploratory Integration: To be fully alive requires being fully engaged. The educational campus can serve as a model for combining the ability to learn, to serve and to be engaged in cultural and recreational activities, all in a pedestrian-scaled environment. These and other insights will bring new life to suburbia.

Five—The Place of Architecture: The architecture of community represents far more than a collection of buildings. The varieties of architectural practice represent an opportunity to work with developers and all other participants toward integrated patterns of town planning that can create public benefits from private investment.

Six—Heroic Commitment: Throughout history those who built with sensitivity and grandeur added something of themselves to the significance of our earthly environment. This is not a matter of *improving* on nature but rather recognizing that we *are* nature.

Seven—Frank Lloyd Wright: The man many regard to have been the world's greatest architect spent a lifetime advocating that the youthful democracy of the United States deserves an architecture of community appropriate to its new spirit of freedom. The result was a concept he called "Broadacre City."

Eight—DC Ranch: This new community in Scottsdale, Arizona is located where the mountains and desert of the Southwest are most beautiful. Its visual and programmatic relationships are arranged with as much care as a composer would give to a symphony.

Nine—The Village of Kohler: This Wisconsin town exists in a category of its own. Few communities have enjoyed its long and continuous history of combining public-sector governance with private-sector guidance. It is a place that has preserved the integrity of its past while making bold commitments to tomorrow.

Ten—Designing the Future: As we enter the 21st century, those of us in the West enjoy unprecedented wealth and freedom along with a global awareness of the successes and failures of others. We have been given an unprecedented opportunity and ability to utilize this awareness to the benefit of our neighborhoods, towns and cities, as well as to the planet we all share and call home.

Examining Our Confusion

ONE

> *"A community is like a ship;*
> *everyone ought to be prepared to take the helm."*
>
> – Henrik Ibsen

Process and Players

This book is all about you. There is no "us" without you, and there can be no community without "us." We are all in this together. The good news is that we are infinitely more able to shape our environments than the present polarity of public discourse would suggest.

If we choose to accept the challenge, our future can be largely a matter of our own making. To move from observer to creator, take a moment to imagine that someone has just knocked on your door to deliver the following message.

Congratulations! Your community has selected you to be its visionary. As part of this selection, you are being granted special powers. You will not only be able to view and understand the earth's current settlement patterns, but you will also be able to turn back the clock, removing all development from the city or region where you live. Your only responsibility will be to put it all back together, providing everything necessary to support the people who are there, plus those who are yet to come. Your great advantage and gift to the future is that you may utilize any and all land-use patterns, transportation systems, building types and architecture that have ever existed throughout history, plus any other provisions that your imagination can create.

Here are a few issues you may wish to consider. When it comes to thinking about transit, remember that there is a difference between mobility and accessibility. Mobility requires only the movement of vehicles. Accessibility requires that people are able to get to where they want to be. You will also want to consider the difference between privacy and community. Humans have a great desire for the former and an equally great need for the latter, but the two impulses can produce results that can seem at odds with each other.

And will you focus on style or performance? For example, many Americans love the look of places like Tuscany and Umbria, but they also love luxurious master bathrooms, bedrooms and kitchens, not to mention their two-, three-, and four-car garages, none of which can be found in the charming places they so admire.

The conflicts continue, for example, between the nostalgia of the little corner store as opposed to the big-box retailers. The problem is that the big boxes tend to have fresher, greater selections, available at lower prices, all of which we demand.

You may also be puzzled as to why people spend billions of dollars to fund mass transit while continuing to rely mainly on their automobiles, or why so many people prefer to commute long distances rather than live closer to where they work. Before you are finished, you will likely realize the privilege of your dictatorial powers as opposed to having to work within the limitations of democracy, codes and human behavior. Here are three introductory discussions to start you on your way.

Technology: Historic settlements have been shaped mainly by the pursuit of security or the creation of wealth. Walled cities were conceived for protection against invaders. The growth of cities around trade routes, seaports, rail lines, airports and freeway interchanges have all been about creating wealth. Common to both motivations is that the earliest forms of communication required personal contact. The growing impact of technology has altered the once dominant need for proximity.

The historic, centralized city-form continues to serve us well, but so do many other settlement patterns. We should at least agree that all dense urban centers are patterned after city shapes that were conceived during periods entirely unlike our own. It would also seem beyond argument that technological advances not only alter what is possible but what is desirable, including the vastly greater choices that can be ours for the asking.

Consensus: The physical development of community is greatly dominated by measurable codes and ordinances, along with the demands of high-volume production and the need for consensus decision-making. Development is also an arena for the less obvious exploration of creative ideas that permit no easy measures and aren't even on speaking terms with the pursuit of consensus.

By its very nature, consensus tends toward simplistic forms of development based on the predictability and comfort of everything being the same—segregated land uses, uniformly sized lots and houses, standardized building heights, the consistent placement of house and lot, and general conformity in the treatment of massing, landscaping and color. From start to finish, for consensus to be achieved, everyone involved in the process—developers, marketing consultants, civil engineers, designers, builders, city officials, realtors and buyers—must all tacitly agree to abide by the same rules.

It isn't that we don't know how to do things a better way, but to do so requires a level of artfulness that can't be legislated and which is not easy to describe. Consensus may carry with it the power of clarity, but it has never been the source of a great painting, or composed a symphony or designed an enduring building. If we truly desire to move forward, we will have to reach for something deeper than simply voting, conducting market studies and focus groups, placing our faith in codes and ordinances, or any other method for lowering our commitments to the common denominator of easy agreement.

Fragmentation: If considered separately, the physical "fragments" that make up the American landscape represent achievements that should be celebrated. We are the envy of the world for our ability to build infrastructure, create flexible office space, design attractive shops and stores, build ever larger religious, recreational and cultural facilities, increase personal mobility, and provide for spacious housing. It is these individual accomplishments that we have concentrated on most—until now.

What we don't much like about development is what its individual pursuits add up to. It is when looking at the totality that our "triumphs" become failures. The puzzling question is, how can we be so critical of what we so obviously desire? For example, our love affair with the automobile, our patronage of ever larger and more entertaining shopping centers, our enjoyment of elegant specialty office complexes, and our revelry in the privacy of our suburban homes. Until we arrive at a deeper understanding as to why we publicly attack what we privately enjoy, we will never be able to move on to a more rewarding future.

Transit and freeway people can fight like the Hatfields and the McCoys, and skirmishes between income groups (especially when they involve considerations for density) are legion. Major urban decisions, such as where to locate a stadium or a shopping center, or even the routing of transit lines can seem more haphazardly political than analytically thoughtful.

Another tendency is to do things the easy way. It may seem that most people, most of the time, will elect to do things the easy way, but the observation is misleading. The greater truth is that human destiny, including its most immediate expression of the marketplace, is not shaped by the "easy" but rather by whatever we understand as best serving our self-interests.

The first step in your role as community visionary will require you to become more genuinely curious about the glaring inconsistencies in public discourse. Among the many paradoxes of modern life is that we are constricting our view as to what works and what doesn't, at the very time when we should be exploring and embracing a broader range of possibilities. Why else would we be repeating such a narrow band of look-alike office buildings, retail centers and housing subdivisions. This constriction coexists with a new level of global awareness that is so dramatic as to seem like a form of time travel. If we wish to broaden our view of the possible, the only way out of this dilemma is to raise the awareness of all parties, and there is no magic wand for doing so. That is why you must now commit yourself to achieving whatever you want to make happen. If development is to move more in the direction that you and others would like to see, the citizens must do their part. All others will surely follow.

One final word of warning—beware of experts. Frank Lloyd Wright considered them to be a blockade to progress. Any time you run into someone who has all the answers, it's more than likely you will be listening to a description of the past. The most valuable participants will not be those who speak with the glibness of authority but those who master the exploratory response to uncertainty.

*"True involvement comes
when the community
and the designer turn
the process of planning
the city into a work of art."*

– Edmund N. Bacon
The Design of Cities

Three Questions to Help Start Our Journey

Which "sprawl" most, older Eastern cities or the auto-oriented, wide-open spaces of the West?

"...many of the densest metropolitan areas in the United States are located in the West—most specifically, in California, Arizona and Nevada. Meanwhile, the older metropolitan areas of the Northeast and Midwest, while their underlying densities are high by national standards, are sprawling far worse than their counterparts elsewhere in the nation."

From 1982 to 1997, which city "sprawled" more, Atlanta or Phoenix?

"Atlanta and Phoenix added very close to the same population—1.36 million additional people in Atlanta, 1.18 million additional people in Phoenix. However, Atlanta urbanized five times as much land to accommodate this additional population as Phoenix did."

If "sprawl" means we are consuming too much land per person, then the solution is to create metropolitan areas with far higher densities. Then during the same 15-year period (1982 to 1997) which city "sprawled" more, New York or Los Angeles?

"New York added 1.13 million persons and urbanized 478,000 acres of land, for a marginal metropolitan density of 2.37 persons per acre, or less than one-third of its overall average in 1982. Los Angeles urbanized a little less land (412,000 acres) but increased its population by more than 3.7 million people—a marginal density of 9.12 persons per acre."

Source: The Brookings Institution Center on Urban and Metropolitan Policy

Defining Sprawl

There is no better way to observe how certainty can interfere with progress than to begin our journey by coming to grips with a single word. It is the word we use most often to express our deep displeasure with growth and development while, at the same time, guaranteeing that we will never understand what we are talking about. The word is sprawl.

Sprawl is an amazing concept. People who are in total disagreement about anything to do with development easily agree that they hate sprawl. The only problem is that there is absolutely no agreement as to what they mean when they use the word. We agree that sprawl is "bad," but because we don't know what it is, we don't know what we want to stop doing. Who sprawls, and what isn't sprawl? Rather than wrestle with such questions, our use of the words "sprawl" and "urban sprawl" become nothing more than confusing and thoughtless name-calling. Three examples illustrate the point.

To persons in rural areas, the threat of sprawl means that other people want to live there as well. They are threatened by the potential development of new houses, office buildings, restaurants, resorts or country clubs—anything that might be built on what is now open land. If existing residents are successful in their opposition, the undeveloped land remains more "owned" by the objectors than those who hold title. Land precluded from new development becomes an open-space amenity for those already there.

The second example involves people who live in subdivisions of large homes on large lots for whom sprawl is anything that isn't an even larger home or at least a larger lot. To such persons, sprawl is higher-density residential, anything commercial, and all things not private, with the greatest offenders being public parks and schools. The obvious dilemma of this view can be seen in surveys that indicate that the two things people hate most are sprawl and density.

The third example is that of the scholars and urban planners whose definition of sprawl is hopscotch, low-density, residential-only development, extending beyond the reach of integrated, close-by shopping, employment, recreational and educational facilities. All this pretty much describes the preferred lifestyle of those in the other two examples.

It is time for all parties to recognize that this standoff is real, and the problem won't go away without acknowledging that sprawl has become the word to describe the look and feel of a broad range of development that increasing numbers of government officials, scholars, design professionals and our most aware citizens simply don't like. And what we don't like has three characteristics: 1) It is the easiest and lowest form of development; 2) It is the most fragmented, and; 3) It is artless. Thus, if we truly oppose sprawl enough to do something about it, we should prepare to master the tasks of creating developments that are complex, comprehensive and artful.

Decentralization

Until we are ready to define sprawl in terms that can be solved, it remains the background music to which we dance a meaningless jig, alternately accusing and defending we know not what. The confusion that gets in the way of pursuing development patterns we might prefer is our failure to acknowledge the difference between the editorial notion of sprawl and the forceful fact of decentralization.

For those who suffer from this confusion, one of the more frequently mentioned causes of sprawl is the Interstate Highway system. While the cause-and-effect connection may seem obvious, this is the kind of reasoning that misses a greater truth. The ability to travel easily and to lessen the time required for transportation and communication has absolutely nothing to do with sprawl and everything to do with decentralization. Anyone who wants to fight the decentralizing force of technology might be just as effective trying to suspend the laws of gravity.

Decentralization is an inexorable trend of civilized life. It started with the establishment of trade routes, followed by sailing ships, steam ships, then continents connected with telegraph lines and nations linked by horse-drawn carriages, rail and the automobile. The direction of the force is always the same, only the technology changes, including the advancement of travel by air, the widespread availability of telephones, radio, television, video-conferencing, the Internet, and now the whole world of wireless, satellite transmission.

The technological evolution won't stop here. None of this need preclude us from choosing to build highly compact cities, but unlike humanity's original reasons for doing so, it won't be because communication is only possible by way of physical proximity.

Are We Returning to the City?

Two very different questions are often asked as though they are the same. The first is, are central cities experiencing a rebirth? The second is, are central cities reversing the trend of people decentralizing into outer areas? The answer to the first is yes. Many more people are moving back to cities, thus fueling their rebirth. The second answer is no. Decentralization continues to be the dominant pattern. Joel Kotkin, Senior Fellow at Pepperdine University's Davenport Institute for Public Policy clarifies the confusion.

"The first dose of reality comes from the demographic trends seen in the 2000 Census. When the numbers were first released, much was made of how many people had decided to make the move into cities. But for every three households that migrated in, five moved out. This outward migration took place most heavily in the critical 35 to 44 age group… Economic growth in the 1990s, like population, flourished not only in the suburbs, but even farther out... The corporate economy is following the same path. The paucity of new urban high-rise towers is one clear indication: despite the economic expansion of the 1990s, only one significant city—Charlotte, North Carolina—saw its skyline transformed."

Sprawl Is Not About Density:
No matter where you live, it is likely that you have heard the notion of sprawl coupled with references to density. This connection between sprawl and density is as meaningless as it is prevalent. These images, along with those on the following two pages, represent a full range of densities. They have only one thing in common—they are all artless development and no matter where in the world they occur, they are all called sprawl.

Artless Development: *It matters little whether streets are straight or curved, or if there are alleys, front porches and "mom-and-pop" shops, sprawl is entirely a matter of the mind-numbing repetition of same-size, same-use components, providing no sculptural form, no visual relief and neither concern nor control over what the repeating elements add up to.*

Exuberance Is Beauty: *For most people, images like these tend to produce a highly pleasurable emotional response. We reach for our cameras to capture some sense of their visual delight. But while they may inspire our admiration, we know better than to try to build such places for ourselves, because in most locations they would be illegal. Settlements like these violate our hillside ordinances, they are denser than what we allow, and their coverage would be seen as excessive. They provide none of the required setbacks, they mix commercial and residential uses, their roadways are too narrow and, most*

egregious of all, they exceed our allowable heights. If you find value in the sanctity of limiting what we build by the generic numbers game, you should be pleased to know that the image on the next two pages represents a text-book example of compliance. It meets every stipulated requirement on the books. From beginning to end, the design and execution of this development was guided by the standards we have put in place to protect our health, safety and welfare. Perhaps it is time to see if this focus on standards shouldn't be opened to consider that artful environments are something we need as well.

Sprawl has little to do with density and everything to do with the production-driven, code-enforced absence of creativity. It is the artless sameness of uniformly sized lots, uniformly massed buildings, monotonously repeating designs and the automobile dependency that inevitably results from the absolute segregation of land uses.

The Facts Don't Always Support Our Preconceptions

Land Use: *"In spite of five centuries of development, urban uses consume only 2.5 percent of the total land area in the United States (1990 Census, Urbanized Area Summary Report). As for the impact of agricultural land conversion, it is noteworthy that the bulk of farmland loss from 1982 to 1992 was the result of a federal conservation program that shifted 32 million acres of cropland to conservation status at a cost of $1.8 billion per year. In contrast, all development in the United States during the same period resulted in the conversion of only 4.1 million acres of cropland (less than 1 percent of the 1982 total). While this loss of farmland was occurring, total farm product increased over 20 percent in real terms and net farm income doubled."*

– J. Thomas Black
Urban Development Consultant

"We are entitled to our own opinions. We are not entitled to our own facts."

– Anonymous

Sprawl: *"For a term in wide use, sprawl has a remarkably slippery definition. It has no accepted yardstick for measurement, and until this year nobody had even attempted to comprehensively measure it. It stands in as a catchall for auto-centered development, scattered housing, strip malls, tract houses and anything else despised by urbanists and environmentalists. But what it is, beyond a convenient term, has been unclear. That might not be a problem: Maybe we can't define sprawl, but we know it when we see it, and it looks a lot like Los Angeles.*

"This year, USA Today *and the Brookings Institution published the results of parallel but competing studies intended to subject sprawl to the rigors of statistical analysis, and among their findings are some serious challenges to conventional thinking on the subject. For starters, taken as a metropolitan region, the five-county Southern California megalopolis of 177 cities that we gather under the term Los Angeles is denser than any other urban region in the continental United States. To be specific, metropolitan Los Angeles uses less land per resident than any other urban region in the lower 48 states (Honolulu alone beats it). And though it has the worst traffic in the nation, it's denser than New York, denser than San Francisco, denser than Chicago (Phoenix is denser than Chicago!), denser than—gasp—Portland, Oregon, the poster child for intelligent growth management. Time for a revision in popular thinking?"*

– *Architecture Magazine*, December 2001

What's Right With These Pictures?

If there weren't a lot to commend developments like this, they wouldn't be so prevalent. Here is why they exist. They are easy to plan, easy to fit within all applicable codes and ordinances, easy to build and easy to sell. Within the walls of each house, the occupants have more privacy and personal space than they ever had before. They can park their cars within steps of their kitchens. Their whole world of "home" is under their control, with no burden of ownership responsibilities for anything beyond their own lot lines.

What's Wrong With These Pictures?

If the statement at the top of the page were all that mattered, we would not have the growing outcries against suburban sprawl. Instead, images like this cause a backlash that threatens the imposition of moratoriums, urban limit lines and the purchase of land to deny development. Billions of dollars are spent by local, state and federal agencies to prohibit such single-purpose developments in favor of a more multifaceted approach to creating community.

Sensory Deprivation: *If our built environments tell us nothing about where we are, in very real terms, we lose an important sense of who we are. It's a face we can't recognize, a song without melody, a place without meaning. If what we see and feel is all about the expedient, both our individual and shared quality and meaning of life is somehow lessened.*

An Artful Context: *If what we see and experience becomes our context of life, complete with recognizable forms, colors, proportions, textures and mystery, such settings enliven our senses. We experience greater meaning because we feel a kinship to all about us. Instinctively, we tap into the story it tells about its unmistakable character and commitment.*

Sprawl	**Creative**
Housing	Neighborhoods
All Private Lots	Shared Open Spaces
Single Density	Varied Densities
Sameness	Diversity
The Look of Process	The Look of Purpose
Static	Emerging
Predictable	Magical
Production Criteria	Human Values
Obvious	Mysterious
Simplistic	Complex
Monotony	Symphony
Generic	Authentic

The Program Sets the Bar

Design and programming are related, but they are not the same. They are the ingredients of the program that determine whether the palette will be rich and varied or constrained and impoverished. For example, if the typical production-driven uniformity that produced suburbia were expressed in musical terms, rather than hearing a melody, it would be like listening to a single note until it drove us all insane.

By contrast, if we were to recreate a hypothetical program that could reasonably underlie the design of the city of York in England, as shown to the right, it would sound something like this. *Take 250 years and build the largest Gothic church in Britain. Surround it with lawns and gardens, provide no areas for parking and keep the streets narrow and few. All housing will be attached, varied in size and shape, and crowned with highly articulated roof forms utilizing a single material in a coordinated range of colors. Last but not least, intermix residential and non-residential uses and make little or no distinction between the character of their appearance.*

Now imagine this same site, but this time its planners, architects and builders are given a program more typical of present-day markets. *Within the next 30 months, design and build an auditorium-style church with 2,000 spaces for surface parking. All houses must be single-family and detached with at least a two-car garage plus surface spaces for guest parking. Place all non-residential uses in a separate zone with each property providing surface parking to accommodate one space per 300 square feet of leasable area. No structure may exceed 30 feet in height above existing natural grade.*

The differences between these two programs are obvious. There will never be a shortage of those who know no better than to use the obvious as an excuse to create the regrettable. Others, on whom the future depends, will use 21st-century tools and insights to explore beneficial relationships between land uses, embrace complexity, change whatever it is about standardization, codes and ordinances that favors mediocrity, find innovative ways of doing more with less, all the while demonstrating the wealth-creating power of cooperation. Using everything from personal commitments, thoughtful design, compelling presentations and strategic marketing, such people are nothing less than society's programmers of a more rewarding and sustainable reality.

Cities or Suburbs

In the world of planning, one is never far from a lively debate as to whether the wave of the future will be on the side of a return to dense urban centers or toward the patterns created by the 140,000,000 Americans who now live in the suburbs. This is a debate none of us should ever want to win, nor should we ignore the dynamic differences between pedestrian-centered core cities and the spacious lure of decentralized living. As author and civic activist Jane Jacobs put it, "Great cities are not like towns, only larger … they are not like suburbs, only denser. They differ from towns and suburbs in basic ways."

Some would argue that New York City is having a hard time being the city Jacobs described. Gentrification and condominiums continue to replace the more people-centered character of organic and distinct neighborhoods. Where there should be easy agreement is that it is no more possible for life lived on an acre in Arizona to be steps away from the diversity and amenities of Manhattan than it is for a New Yorker to be steps away from the exotic vegetation and atmospheric effects of the Sonoran Desert. Vive la différence!

The most beneficial opportunities of the 21st century require that we replace our tendency toward "either/or" thinking with a deeper understanding of the varied expressions of community. Simplistic formulas, along with the dumbing-down of citizen dialogue, have produced look-alike structures on look-alike streets in look-alike cities and towns. By comparison to the more diverse and engaging images on these two pages, the one-size-fits-all approach to development has had its day and it wasn't pretty.

What Isn't Sprawl: *These settlements are each widely varied and highly complex. No matter what their respective densities, the absence of sprawl can be clearly felt in terms of character. It is a convincing look of purpose. It isn't necessary to know the function of these structures to observe that each, in its own way, houses the provisions of community. They do so with a sense of proportion, grace and charm— all ingredients that exist far beyond the reach of arguing "for" or "against" whatever is being debated at the moment.*

Automobiles and Transit

Of all the complex issues involved in the design of cities, the debate between designing to accommodate the automobile as opposed to an urban form that favors group transit is the most formative, emotional and thoroughly puzzling of all. Arguments in favor of the automobile concern individual choice, freedom, comfort, safety and convenience. Those in favor of transit espouse a completely different set of advantages, including the conservation of land and energy as a result of the denser, more compact settlement patterns required to make group transport effective. Those who oppose great expenditures for transit often live in low-density areas, where they feel that what works well in other areas, or in the past in all areas, is now nothing but costly and thinly disguised social engineering. Those who support transit almost always insist that all automobile-centered settlements are unsustainable.

To get beyond this impasse we might start by agreeing on at least the following seven observations.

1 None of us enjoys automobile congestion, other than to acknowledge that all the greatest cities of the world have it, nor are we particularly fond of the look of garage doors and massive parking lots, either empty or full.

2 Freeways are physical barriers to the fabric of community and are generally not as pleasurable as driving on beautiful country roads. If by some magic, we could function equally well without them, freeways might not be missed. However, we might also agree that nothing is known that can provide the same individual service as the automobile, and for distance travel, that means something other than gridded streets with endless intersections. To send cars and trucks through neighborhood streets, rather than limited-access arteries, is bad planning.

3 Not only did Henry Ford succeed in his goal to "democratize the automobile," there was also a fairly well-documented conspiracy that worked to destroy public transportation by downgrading its quality of service. But that was then, and it had little to do with the ongoing force of decentralization. Those who first settled in the suburbs of Chicago, for instance, traveled by train.

4 Rightly or wrongly, if the most compelling arguments against the use of automobiles are about the inefficiencies of personal over group transport, then won't we one day be making the same argument against private boats, aircraft and, eventually, the "private" single-family dwelling?

5 Rather than going down that road, can't we simply agree that a successful future will demand that we create more artful relationships between that which is to our advantage to "own" and that which is in our best interests to "use?"

6 Whatever else we may decide, it is beyond argument that the United States is steeped in a car culture of which California is its flagship. California drivers spend more than 315,000 hours a day stuck in traffic. One

Californian, explaining the need for a beautiful car, put it this way, "Even if you are trying to save the planet, you have got to look good while you are doing it."

7 The sometimes irreverent, always searching character of the American spirit will never stop looking for new forms of community as appropriate to the 21st century as the central city was to the needs and opportunities of the past. If we can conceive of relationships that better support our needs, this could lead to cities or portions of cities designed to function entirely without cars or trucks.

Evaluating Transit

One of the most comprehensive advocacies for transit is presented in *Sustainability and Cities: Overcoming Automobile Dependencies* by Peter Newman and Jeffrey Kenworthy. The following four paragraphs are quoted directly from their findings.

"U.S. and Australian cities are the most extensive in their dependence on the automobile, as shown by their transportation patterns, infrastructure and land use. Canadian cities are less automobile-dependent, with better transit and greater integration of land use. European cities are three to four times less automobile-dependent than U.S. cities in terms of automobile use, infrastructure, and land-use intensity. Wealthy Asian cities (Singapore, Hong Kong and Tokyo) are eight times less automobile-dependent than U.S. cities. However, the newly industrializing Asian cities (Bangkok, Jakarta, etc.) are showing a marked and rapidly growing automobile orientation in their transportation patterns and infrastructure,

and although fringe land uses are developing greater auto-orientation, their overall land-use patterns are still dense and strongly favor transit and non-motorized modes.

"Automobile use is increasing in all but a few cities (Stockholm and Zurich), but there are large differences in rates of growth. U.S. cities grew the most despite predictions that suburbanization of work would slow down car use. Transit use increased in all cities despite predictions of its demise globally. Spectacular increases in Europe continue to set the benchmark. Density patterns indicate an historic reversal is occurring globally, with increases or reversal of declines evident nearly everywhere. Inner-city growth is much more evident than in previous periods except in U.S. cities, where density increases are mostly occurring in outer suburban 'edge cities,' that are heavily auto-dependent.

"Automobile-dependent Australian and U.S. cities use 12 to 13 percent of their city wealth on their passenger transportation systems; Canadian and European cities use 7 to 8 percent; wealthy Asian cities use 5 percent; and more automobile-oriented, newly industrializing Asian cities use 15 percent of their city wealth on transportation. The implication for sustainability is that reducing automobile dependence is good for the economy of cities.

"The best examples of reducing automobile dependence are to be found in European cities, especially Stockholm, Copenhagen, Zurich and Freiburg, with continuing success being shown by wealthy Asian cities like Singapore, Hong Kong and Tokyo, and selected poorer cities, such as Curitiba in Brazil. In Canada, Toronto

and Vancouver have shown some good signs, which are reflected in significantly better land use and transportation characteristics than in U.S. or Australian cities. In the United States, Boulder, Portland and Boston are showing that tackling automobile dependence can begin even in the world's most automobile-oriented nation, with a range of positive results, such as more compact housing, a more vital public realm, revitalization of central and inner areas, and better transit systems."

Newman and Kenworthy provide exhaustive data to support their findings, yet the extent to which Americans believe that fixed rail transit is a matter for our future or our past continues to vary widely. Perhaps we could all agree on something more basic. To argue against public transportation is foolish, but to jump to arguing in favor of light rail where its limitations make it unsuitable for the present and future land-use relationships to be served is even more foolish.

Couldn't we also agree that even those cities like Paris with the world's most comprehensive transit systems also have streets filled to capacity? Simply stated, those who can drive, do. And in the densest areas of Manhattan, those vehicles that make the streets look like flowing ribbons of yellow may be called taxis, but they are still automobiles. Those who use them may not own a car, but they are still auto-dependent.

"One reason why mass transit underperforms so often in the United States is that it is often employed as an ideological tool. Urbanist civic leaders and planners make an initial policy decision that a metropolitan area needs "public transit." Nowadays that automatically seems to mean some kind of rail, still almost invariably focused on the downtown, like 19th-century streetcar lines. From the outset, transportation planning thus becomes an exercise to justify preordained hardware... Outside of densely developed cities like New York and Chicago, no American public transportation system even remotely equals the personal convenience and efficiency of the private automobile."

– Tom Martinson
American Dreamscape:
The Pursuit of Happiness in
Postwar Suburbia

Automobiles and Rail: *There need be no argument between the two. Plan for rail wherever there are great concentrations of people who are able to travel at scheduled times between fixed locations. When the need is to operate at all scales, from the neighborhood to the regional, from wherever we are to wherever we want to be, at any time we wish, nothing compares to the automobile. And no matter what the mode of transportation, wherever the hardware is most condensed, no form of high-capacity, high-speed system is likely to be the place to look for community charm.*

Transit's Three Hurdles

We might conclude that the United States is behind the older European and Asian cultures. Another view would be that the use of transit is increasing where there is no other choice and the use of automobiles is increasing where choice is not only possible, but of paramount importance to users.

For light-rail transit to be effectively introduced in low- to mid-density areas traditionally dominated by the automobile, there are three very different but mutually dependent hurdles—the most obvious being the political will and ability to take on the single largest financial burden such cities have ever faced. The second hurdle is to revolutionize the community's land patterns in order to create a mixture of uses while greatly increasing residential densities. The third hurdle is to create a physical network and culture that make walking highly desirable.

Whether for private or public objectives, it is common for the more refined elements of any proposal to be thwarted because, "We can't afford it." Ironically, when it comes to introducing transit to growing cities, of the three hurdles, funding may be the easiest to get over. Here is how it works. Increased traffic volumes cannot be swept under the rug—they are visual, personal and emotional. Congestion is almost guaranteed to rise to the top of everyone's list of complaints about city services. The city's leaders, amplified by the local press, eventually guide this outcry into a bond issue. While the ultimate investment is huge and beyond most people's imaginations,

great care is taken to craft the routing of the system as well as its funding mechanisms to achieve a positive vote. The result is to understate the pain while over-promising for the hoped-for gains.

This leaves the other two hurdles. Unlike passing a bond issue, which requires nothing more than the abstraction of a majority vote, the other two hurdles (which are really one) strike at the heart of the most personally involved aspects of human choice. Now we are talking about how and where we live. When it comes to giving up our automobiles, the more difficult questions are not ones of mobility or transport but pleasure, convenience and privacy. As reported by Anthony Downs of the Brookings Institution, there is a reason why a 1995 personal transit study indicated that more than 90 percent of all commuters in the United States used private automobiles, while only 3.5 percent used public transit. And of the total number of transit users, somewhere between 22 and 35 percent were located in New York City.

Those who are at the forefront of transit-oriented designs (TODs) routinely state that the gross densities required to make mass transit effective is in the realm of 15 to 30 units (houses or apartments) per acre. How many cities would like to include that candid criterion in their bond issue language, when asking their low-density-loving citizens to spend 50 million dollars or more per mile for light rail? When communities decide to jump on the bandwagon of public transit, they should at least own up to the fact that the trend is going the opposite way.

From 1960 to 1995, the number of people driving to work increased 30 percent while the use of transit continued to decline. None of this should deter us in the slightest from creating more effective and efficient land-use relationships for greater accessibility in order to reduce the number of passenger miles driven. What is needed, however, is a deeper understanding of cause and effect. As with all aspects of creating community, success will not result from simplistic, single-purpose pursuits. The same thoughtlessness surrounding our use of the word "sprawl" erupts when the subject has anything to do with transportation. Both proponents of transit and defenders of the automobile seem to find it easier to choose sides than consider the place of each in an overall system.

The sooner we accept that a system designed to use whatever "hardware" best suits our varying needs, the sooner we will be able to plan accordingly. Otherwise we will simply continue playing our zero-sum games in which the only possible victory may be nothing more than replacing a lane of vehicles with a dedicated artery for light rail. Depending upon a host of other considerations, this could either help or hinder the desired objective.

If every ground-transportation vehicle, including trains, streetcars, buses, vans, automobiles, bicycles and feet—as well as present and future specialty vehicles for personal travel—were seen as nothing but tools for accessibility, we would understand that, like all tools, we should use each one for whatever it does best.

A first step in thinking about land uses organized around a multi-modal transportation system is to differentiate between the most idealized means of travel within each of three zones. The smallest, within a 10-minute walk, could be dominantly pedestrian. The next, within a 10-mile ride or drive, would be bicycles, automobiles, vans and taxis. And as long as the proper densities are either planned or in place, buses and light rail could be used to connect and traverse the region and the other two zones. The automobile will continue to be used in all zones, but proper planning can result in decreasing both the length and frequency of trips.

Using What We Have

It would be the height of folly to think that any single fact or even a whole book of facts could bring us into agreement concerning the roles of automobiles and transit. But what we can do is move away from promoting vested interests to a more comprehensive and shared understanding of the connection between how we want to live and how we get about. As a clue to something we may want to do better, according to the U.S. Department of Transportation, the average American spends twice the time driving as they do with their children.

We will need to move beyond making unhelpful distinctions between the use of automobiles and the use of transit. Assuming that we favor the car but that mass transit would be a more responsible choice is like telling people to take a cold shower because it's good for you.

Rather than forcing society to go back to high-density cities or to neighborhoods of the 1920s, with their pre-automobile dominance of street cars, why not look at ways to better use other forms of personal transit, including automobiles, motor-scooters and bicycles.

- For activities that would pose no injury to residential settings, instead of precluding live/work relationships with restrictive zoning, aggressively encourage and facilitate their further development.

- Instead of a garage full of different vehicles (America has more cars than drivers) make it routine and easy to access short-term rentals of all types of vehicles to suit our activities on a case-by-case basis.

- For those whose needs are infrequent or who are too young, too old or otherwise unable to drive, it would be more effective to use taxis and on-call vans as forms of "targeted transit" than to rely on often-empty buses.

- Less familiar but already in widespread use are taxis and vans that operate with the same fixed-route predictability as buses but in more specifically defined areas.

- We will soon see more widespread use of pooled cars. This organized car-sharing movement began in Europe and is now spreading across the United States.

- For both large-scale development and the eventual retrofitting of suburbia, treat all of the above considerations as if they were as basic to the design as any other component of the infrastructure.

It Will Always Be Personal: *The sooner we acknowledge that mass transit will never eliminate our desire for personal mobility, the sooner we will get behind innovations that do more with less–providing more mobility with less bulk and greater fuel economy with less pollution. Major auto-makers, along with architects, designers and inventors, are all getting into the act. While we will never give up our demand for transportation that is always ready, safe, convenient and personal, we will design more fuel-efficient, ecologically friendly vehicles and new propulsion systems, including devices for levitation.*

Living and Moving About

History indicates a surprisingly limited variety of housing types, settlement patterns and transportation systems. The adjoining lists make no distinction between small or large dwellings as opposed to those for seasonal use. Under transportation, there are no distinctions regarding fuel types.

In the evolution of community design, what we deal with mainly are the relationships between the various ingredients, and in all cases, we must face the daunting variables of human behavior. There may be scholarly objection to listing only 11 forms of individual shelter and settlement patterns and 14 methods of transportation throughout history, but there should be little or no argument about what the lists reveal.

In planning the future, rather than looking for any "silver bullets" of technology, our most significant achievements are more likely to be found within the human subtleties of how we design our relationships to each other and with the land that we share.

SHELTER

Cave
Moveable tents
Mobile homes
Detached houses
Attached houses
Apartments and flats
High-rise dwellings
Houseboats
Shop-houses
Dormitories
Space stations

SETTLEMENTS

Nomadic
Walled cities
Centralized cities
Suburban
Rural
Gated communities
Farms
Ranches
Plantations
Campuses
Congregate care

TRANSPORTATION

Walking
Animals
Pulled or carried carts
Bicycles
Trains
Boats
Automobiles/trucks
Elevators
Airplanes
Moving sidewalks
Buses
Cable cars
Monorails
Orbiting craft

Imprisoned by Numbers

Nothing provokes more certainty than arguments involving anything that can be quantified. In the realm of land use, most disagreements center around 12 measures: 1) Density; 2) Height; 3) Setbacks; 4) Open space; 5) Water consumption; 6) Light-reflective values; 7) Night lighting; 8) Automobile trips per day; 9) Noise; 10) Building area; 11) Coverage; and 12) Parking. Common to each category is its ability to be represented by a number, and almost any number can be a spark for outrage.

This numerical view carries with it the appearance of exactitude that can be used to support what may be nothing but uninformed opinion. The loss that results from a focus on such simplistic absolutes is that it discourages anything not already defined by whatever is considered the norm. But what about the special-case opportunities that long-term players may wish to explore, all in the direction of something better? Codes and ordinances, as well as those who use them as a substitute for thought, are every bit as aggressive in precluding excellence as they are in their attempts to protect society from abuse. Intended or not, when formulated decision-making prevails, highly desirable accomplishments that might have been, become impossible to even consider. And for every highly publicized defeat, there are countless other proposals that will never even be tried. The result is a wholesale surrender of creative design to standards for which the overriding objective of the enforcers is to never make a decision that hasn't already been made or memorialized by code.

It is not uncommon for near-vicious battles to erupt over whether a proposed rezoning should be allowed to have one or two additional units per acre, while other places on earth have densities with a hundred times that amount or more, and now the rubric of "new urbanism" is applied to settlement patterns that are neither new nor urban.

To plan for better, more sustainable land uses, it will be necessary to think of broadening our range of acceptable measures. For example, one density is not "better" than another, only different, and if we know that a city has a transit system, that doesn't tell us whether we are talking about Paris or Calcutta. If we are told it has a population of approximately 12 persons per acre, we wouldn't know if the reference was to Detroit or Garden Grove, California. Similarly, if we know the density is 24 persons per acre, we could be talking about Jersey City, New Jersey or San Francisco. So why do we focus on such measures rather than on the more significant character and relationships? We do so for the same reason that we build fragmented, single-purpose suburbia—it's easier.

How we plan for land use or for transportation should never be considered independently of the other. If we are to encourage more thoughtful patterns of development, the first step will be to guarantee that the review and approval process favors informed understanding of operational realities over the reckless opinions that have so easily dominated public debate.

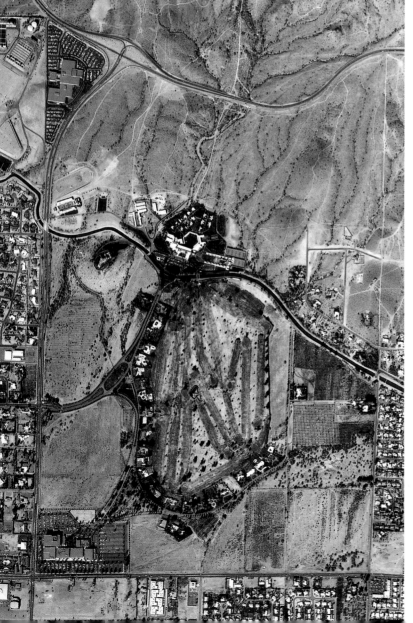

Arizona Biltmore Estates

Lessons of Time

When the famed Arizona Biltmore Hotel was dedicated on February 23, 1929, it was four miles outside Phoenix city limits. It had its own water system designed to serve the needs of the hotel and a few adjoining estates. Nearly a half century later, I became engaged in planning the 1,040 acres of undeveloped land surrounding the hotel. The resultant Biltmore master plan was regarded to be the largest and most significant rezoning in the city's history. It took three people to carry the documents into city hall and two television stations were on hand to cover the official filing.

Months before the plan was filed, four Phoenix city council members announced their opposition. The city staff's 51-page report recommended denial of the overall master plan as well as every one of its 41 separate requests for rezoning. The heads of the city's parks, transportation and planning departments each gave interviews to the press stating their opposition. On October 31, 1974, the headline of the afternoon paper announced that the plan had been denied. The next day, a follow-up story in *The Arizona Republic* was headlined, "Planning Board Urges Rejection of Brilliant Biltmore Plan." No one denied that the plan was good, it was just that "the proposed changes for the area were just too great."

History has shown these concerns to be short-sighted. They reflected nothing but an inability to imagine the emerging future of what is now the sixth-largest city in the nation and growing daily. In spite of overwhelming opposition, the Phoenix city council gave its unanimous approval. The 1973 critics of the plan were absolutely certain about two things— the plan was "too dense," and it would "destroy property values."

The property, as shown on these and the next two pages, is now fully built out. Not only is it the least dense development in the area, its own property values have skyrocketed, and it has been the catalyst for creating the most highly valued urban core in the entire city.

In place of what would have been the monolithic sameness of one-acre lots, there is now a wide range of housing, from relatively small units to some of the most expensive estates in the metropolitan area. The promise of the plan has been fulfilled with employment, resort, recreational and commercial activities. A historic flooding problem was resolved by a series of six retention lakes, and the only major landscaped open space to exist anywhere along one of the city's most highly developed arterials was provided.

Our Living
Laboratory

TWO

"The community stagnates without the impulse of the individual. The impulse dies away without the sympathy of the community."

– William James

Individuality and Community

The built environment, consisting of the tools, places, and events that have been designed, organized and created to support daily life, comprises humanity's most telling record of its needs, dreams and desires. It is also the clearest demonstration of what was believed to be achievable at any moment in history. These well-documented patterns have continued to change over time with one of the most significant changes being the possibility for individuals to live away from the group. In the transition from nomadic tribes to agricultural settlements, then industrial villages and now information-based economies, the distance factor has been altered by the measure of time. When we are able to communicate at the speed of light, it changes the need for proximity. Some have called it "the death of distance."

The Desire for Privacy

Never in human history have people been more able to live in patterns of isolation. We have invented nearly every imaginable device in order to be able to live alone. The automobile allows us to traverse entire cities in personal and hermetically sealed enclosures. It is no longer necessary to walk among others in search of a public phone or to do our banking. The Internet allows for intimate "chats" without ever seeing or being seen by anyone else in the conversation. Low-density suburbia—now the dominant pattern of new development—allows millions of people to "live" within a few feet of each other without ever having to meet, and the same is true for people who live above one another in far denser high-rise apartments.

The Need for Community

Whether for altruistic reasons or just plain old-fashioned self-interest, increasing numbers of people are concluding that the best way to achieve a degree of privacy is to pay equal attention to the shared consequences of our individual actions.

For the majority of development since World War II, the human paradox of privacy and community has been played out like two sides of a warring assault, with the sterile look of suburbia being the recorded triumph of privacy over community. We have built it and lived it, and now we want something more. We have reached what inventor, architect, engineer, mathematician, poet and cosmologist Buckminster Fuller described when he said, "Unity is at a minimum two." Although we may not always see it that way, light and shade, hot and cold, convex and concave, compression and tension always and only coexist. We are approaching the realization that for privacy and community to be at their best, they too must coexist.

Embracing Change

It doesn't take a great deal of imagination to acknowledge that the passage of a few thousand years can bring about dramatic change. But what about the dynamics of things going on around us right now? We are all guilty of paying lip service to the inevitability of change as the normal unfolding of life, while acting as though everything will stay just as it exists now.

This denial is not only true for individuals who openly oppose change, but also for those whose tasks it is to imagine and design realities that are yet to be. The citizen who fights change clings to the familiarity of how everything looks today. Architects and planners who might seem to be advocating change hold on to their plans and renderings to show how everything will look when "finished."

"Given a choice between changing or proving that change isn't necessary, most people get busy on the proof."
– John Kenneth Galbraith

"The only immutable law is the law of change."
– Heraclitus

Add to this the dramatic increase in the use of legal covenants, conditions and restrictions (CC&Rs) that memorialize the present into patterns of perpetuity, that preclude all manner of adjustments that might be both wise and necessary for future success. This endeavor to arrest change is anti-life.

In the design of communities, it is only if we limit our vision to a very brief time frame, say, a generation or two, that things can appear to be static. In reality, a community is a living system involving continuous recycling from birth to death to life, and on and on.

How then should we view change? Without being any less committed to the present, a good first step would be to acknowledge that the future will not only permit but depend on others to re-use, rekindle and, in some cases, entirely replace what we have done.

To acknowledge this as both inevitable and welcome will help focus our attention on matters that are more likely to stand the test of time, instead of on the hairsplitting criteria of codes, ordinances or voguish notions of style.

Grow or Die

Do the individuals who design, build and occupy new structures ever picture them abandoned and in decay? That isn't likely, and for the most part it isn't necessary, because humans tend to have a shorter life span than buildings. Plus, unlike humans, buildings can periodically be made as new as when they were first constructed. But change is always taking place, which is, after all, how small settlements become major cities.

"Most visions for the future,
if studied carefully,
read more like a fairly accurate
description of the present."

– Herman Kahn

"Learn to see in the abstract, but not so
abstract that you lose your
usefulness to society."

– Frank Lloyd Wright

Visionary Relevance

The above quotations are excellent bookends for anyone who seeks to be an effective visionary. If we try to be relevant, we are likely to, as futurist Herman Kahn suggested, offer nothing more than a thinly disguised account of the present. If, on the other hand, our notions about planning and designing for the future try to take into account tectonic shifts, we will likely lose our usefulness to the time and place where we are able to add something of value.

No one can predict the future, but for centuries people have been designing it. Everything we cause to happen today ripples out to form tomorrow's effects. It is neither possible nor necessary to know precisely what such effects and consequences will be in order to have an intuitive sense of judgment. If today's decisions are simplistic, timid, confused and expedient, we can't expect that sustainable elegance and greatness will one day spring up and shock us out of our wits. On the other hand, if we act boldly in the direction of what we can perceive to be a more desirable future, we can expect to reap the rewards.

If for no other reason than to practice thinking beyond the more evident patterns of yesterday, why not make a list of observations to stimulate our ability to visualize the future? Here are seven to get us started.

- It is unlikely that those living during any period of history were clearly aware of what they were part of becoming. This is equally true for all of us.

- Developers will continue the practice of learning from each other, but they will become increasingly interested in mainstreaming some of the more individualistic and custom approaches that were easy to ignore during the suburban heyday of being able to sell anything they could produce.

- So-called "new urbanism," especially those elements that are a reversion to the developmental patterns of the 1920s, will come to be regarded as more quaint or picturesque than anything significant for the future.

- The difference between the design of one's office and home will lessen, along with the diminishing difference between work and life. People will increasingly work out of their homes, and they will design where they live to support what they do, much like the historic integration of family ranches, farms and plantations. Zoning ordinances will be revised to not only permit what most now prohibit, but to aggressively encourage a far greater sense of integration.

- The sameness of suburban patterns of the last half century is having its last fling, especially since the traditional nuclear family of two parents and two children is the fastest declining category in the nation. Some project that our fastest growing group households, made up of multiple families living together, could exceed 15 percent of the total by 2010.

- Another familiar pattern that could be reaching its peak is the hermetically sealed skyscraper with its look-alike floors. The one- and two-story structures of suburbia, together with the old form of high-rise, will morph into richly complex, multi-terraced structures that permit a holistic integration of uses, with more direct exposure to light, air and gardens. This will occur mainly in the land-rich areas of the West, less so in the East, and not at all in the highly constrained areas of older central cities.

- Rather than thinking of "urban limit lines" as temporary holding patterns to control growth, we will establish regional open-space networks framed by edges as inviolate as the shorelines of the Great Lakes. In addition to areas defined by natural features, the regional networks will be designed to provide connective corridors that meander in and around all areas of present and future development.

In all of these examples, the line between vision and relevance is as thin as the eye of a needle. To move a little in either direction can thwart opportunity. The most effective visions for the 21st century will combine the accumulated experience of others with our own record of trial and error. Our awareness has never been greater, nor have our tools and opportunities for making good things happen ever been more spectacular. The newest force of all is humanity's appetite for things, places and experiences beyond anything known to the past. These desires are sweeping the world's institutions with a tidal wave of influences that won't be denied.

The old frontiers were all about quantity and territory. The new frontiers are all about quality and doing more with less. To give our best to the future requires that we nurture these new tendencies in the direction of the ultimate human luxury—to live, learn and love in the creative vitality of community.

More Visionary Than Relevant

Paolo Soleri calls his structures "arcologies," a word made by combining the words architecture and ecology. While it is unlikely that he will ever witness the completion of Arcosanti, shown to the right in the Arizona desert, it is utterly astonishing that one man has been able to carry his vision as far as he has.

Yet he has been more successful getting scholarly and journalistic acclaim than he has in bringing his concepts to fruition. There are many reasons for this, one of which is that he has elected to be more visionary than relevant. He preaches an "either/or" gospel in which we either abandon our patterns of living and move into an "arcology" or disregard him altogether.

For anyone involved in traditional development, what Soleri proposed would be difficult to entertain as a viable alternative. Far easier to envision would be his structures one day replacing the familiar skyscrapers that cast shadows on each other or cause extreme glare with reflections off their glass façades.

Humanity could easily conclude that to continue building single-use, hermetically-sealed skyscrapers totally dependent on mechanical systems for life-support is unsafe, undesirable and unhealthy. Soleri's pioneering work might then lead others to achieve a sculptural variety of mixed-use urban densities consisting of terraced and trellised space, flooded with natural light and air, surrounded by multi-level gardens, groves and orchards, some of which could be designed for both pleasure and safety, stepping down to the surrounding countryside.

Doing More With Less

To the student of community, every aspect of life raises questions for which the answers are always beyond easy reach. In addition to the lessons we can learn from our own experience, our living laboratory has five dominant sources for learning from the experience of others: 1) Environmental expressions of community left by past civilizations, as discussed in Chapter Six; 2) Coexistent patterns of emergent communities in places and circumstances entirely unlike our own; 3) Commitments of individuals and groups seeking something other than what the conventional marketplace provides; 4) Innovative designs for highly custom but low-cost structures; and 5) Special-purpose programs in special places. None of the examples that follow are readily transferable, but all have deeper lessons that can inspire further insights of our own.

Emergent Communities

It has been common for those of us in the West to refer to the "Third World" or "the undeveloped nations" with emotions ranging from pity and wariness to revulsion and ignorance. Lynne Twist, who is quoted on this page, is a proud and beautiful woman whose life of purpose and meaning has been centered almost entirely around these so-called undeveloped nations, but her view is quite different. She sees what she calls "the less consuming nations" as caldrons of strength from which the West can learn a great deal about the commitment of community. Rather than thinking of such places as primal versions of our own experiences, a more authentic view is to see human beings very much like ourselves experiencing and adapting to a variety of circumstances that are thoroughly centered on community for success.

The scenes on the next two pages are of Hong Kong, India, Vietnam and South Africa. What is most useful for our purposes is to observe the richness of the practical elements of daily life—including everything from multi-use activities of simple spaces to the spontaneous spirit of color, beauty and interaction between people in which there is little difference between devotion, commerce and leisure.

An observable pattern in Western culture is that affluence breeds a desire for comfort, as well as a tendency toward privacy and separation. While it may seem normal for us to understand life as occurring mainly in private places, approximately 80 percent of the world's population exhibits a natural tendency toward living more integrated lives in dominantly public places. The 1.4 billion of us who enjoy relative affluence are not going to give up our pursuit of what we consider to be the "good life," but we will become increasingly aware of the earth's 4.6 billion people who live very differently from us and from whom there is much that we can learn.

"Part of what happens in life is that we categorize. There's service over here, work over there, family over here, and then people are always struggling with having things get more balanced. When you have found or allowed yourself to discover that which your life is about, you don't need to work on balance. You live a life of integrity, which means wholeness and completeness. Everything you do is imbued with the power and beauty of life itself."

– Lynne Twist

Seeing Beyond Ourselves: *A good way to learn from circumstances unlike our own is to look for ways in which people have been able to do more with less. While the physical structures in these images range from modest to none, the human interaction is a seamless celebration of everything from people who may not even know each other exercising together in a public square, to displays of pots, fresh fruits and a floating marketplace. In each example, it is not someone's notion of thematic entertainment but rather basic provisions for life that result in a lively and colorful sense of community.*

*"Our most basic common link is that we
all inhabit this planet. We all breathe the
same air. We all cherish our children's
future. And we are all mortal."*

– John F. Kennedy

A New Generation of Developers

Much has been written about cohousing or the making of deliberate neighborhoods and communities. More often than not such writing focuses on the lives of the individuals who join together to participate in some form of communal living. Equally interesting is that cohousing represents an alternative delivery system for creating the built environment. Because cohousing is a customized process, it changes the ground rules for what is possible to achieve. The scale of cohousing has been too small and complex to be of interest to conventional developers, thus the participants have been directly engaged in everything from land acquisition to programming, rezoning, design and construction. Instead of anything formulaic, the entire process is far more personal, involving a great deal of caring, commitment and passion.

"Nice idea. You'll never do it here."
Those were the discouraging words that greeted the South Mountain Company as it began its quest to build affordable housing, plus its own headquarters, on beautiful Martha's Vineyard. Employing a collaborative method involving all parties, the company was not only able to overcome the restrictive zoning for its project, but the town has since adopted a number of innovative standards that encourage more thoughtful and affordable housing. Called "Island Cohousing," the Martha's Vineyard community consists of 16 houses clustered around a pedestrian commons, with all cars kept at the perimeter. The residents themselves created the community to fit how they wanted to live, including the shared use of a common house, pond and gardens.

"Above all we need, particularly as children, the reassuring presence of a visible community, an intimate group that enfolds us with understanding and love, and that becomes an object of our spontaneous loyalty, as a criterion and point of reference for the rest of the human race."

– Lewis Mumford

Designing for Life: *Top left photo is the Bakken Cohousing Community in Horsholm, Denmark, which consists of 25 houses with a 5000-square-foot common house. The above and center photos are of cohousing on Martha's Vineyard. To the left is South Mountain Company's shop and office building, situated as an integral and compatible feature of the residential community.*

> *"There can be no vulnerability without risk; there can be no community without vulnerability; there can be no peace, and ultimately no life, without community."*
>
> – M. Scott Peck

Custom Neighborhoods

Unlike conventional development, which is shaped by "expert" notions of generalized market segments, cohousing is designed around the dreams of specific individuals. In conventional development, market segments are defined by considerations for attracting the broadest range of buyers, where choices can be made as uniformly simple as possible. The mass builder seldom thinks about individual desires and values, especially those that may be more personal and holistic. But when viewed from the perspective of individuals, it is not surprising that objectives go beyond being shoehorned into someone else's limited definitions of "market segments." Rather than just purchasing a house, they want to take part in the design of their lives, including the advantages of a custom home extended to that of a custom neighborhood. The site plan is of the Martha's Vineyard Community.

> *"To create buildings and settings that will be loved and admired for generations, that honor craft, that strive to respect nature, and that learn from the past while anticipating the future."*
>
> – From the South Mountain Company's
> Mission Statement

EcoVillage Cohousing Cooperative: Ithaca, N.Y.

Cohousing's Future

Existing communities typically cluster from 12 to 35 homes around some form of common facilities. Residents participate in the planning and design process to ensure that the resultant community will meet their needs. Each household owns a private residence—complete with kitchen—but also shares common facilities which may include a dining room, children's playrooms, workshops, guestrooms, vegetable gardens, a swimming pool, spa and fitness areas. In most cases, the residents take responsibility for the management and organization as necessary to meet their ongoing and changing needs. Cohousing for the future will take new forms and be known by other names.

Such developments will occur in response to already existing trends. The motivation for these more customized communities (at all price ranges) will be to take advantage of doing more with less by way of cooperation and commitment beyond that which produced the suburban developments of the past. The cohousing developments that now exist around the world represent an exploration of ideas that will evolve into more widespread opportunities. The heart of cohousing is its greater level of societal cooperation, without which sprawling suburbia may be the best we can do. Even a slightly greater degree of trust and cooperation will open the floodgates for doing things a better way.

Community of Patio Homes: *In keeping with the builder's need for standardization, La Luz, a complex in New Mexico, consists of a series of repeating units. What is different is that everything about the design has been carefully considered to highlight views and environmental conditions specific to the site. Provisions for indoor/outdoor living are centered on a series of shared pedestrian courtyards that enhances both the character of individuality and community. Three decades after it was first constructed, this creative complex remains highly valued by its residents and as architecturally timeless as its natural setting. Differing greatly from that which influenced the design of New England settlements, as shown in the next chapter, La Luz pays homage to the historic precedents of the Southwest without resorting to imitation.*

Low-Cost and Brilliant

Countering the architectural dialogue that gravitates toward elitist jargon, Samuel Mockbee would tell his students that what they designed had to be "warm, dry and noble." Mockbee's work epitomized doing more with less by way of design. His genius combined the use of imaginative systems and techniques, the utilization of readily available or overlooked materials and methods for building with

cooperation. What he demonstrated for both housing and his designs for shared multi-use facilities is the kind of caring creativity that will become increasingly required for humanitarian success. The lessons to be learned from Samuel Mockbee's work are many. Most of all, it is a convincing and inspiring demonstration of the triumph of brilliance over circumstance.

Design at Its Best: *Architectural excellence, especially that which is deemed worthy of being published, is often characterized by exotic forms, space, structure and materials. And when articles appear concerning low-income housing or other subsidized development, the emphasis is generally on process—for example, governmental programs or volunteer initiatives like Habitat for Humanity. The late Samuel Mockbee and his students at Auburn University united these accomplishments by designing imaginative buildings for communities in some of Alabama's poorest settlements. These images and those on the following two pages represent his creative use of scavenged materials, from colored bottles, waste cardboard and bales of hay, to discarded concrete rubble, old tires, automobile windshields, and salvaged bricks and lumber.*

'For the last couple of decades, you could safely presume that any architect who focused his or her talents on helping the poor did so at the expense of design. Indeed, it has often seemed as if social consciousness and aesthetics were linked in a zero-sum game: if you cared passionately about one, it was almost a given that you didn't care as much about the other. Samuel Mockbee's gift was how completely he transcended that equation. It didn't exist in his life, and it didn't exist in his career. Mockbee, who died at the age of 57, made art, and he made buildings that poor people needed, and they were one and the same.''

– Paul Goldberger
Architecture Magazine, March 2002

Community as Adaptive Re-Use

The Convent of San Francesco in Cetona, Italy was first built in 1212. It is now a community dedicated to the care and rehabilitation of young drug addicts and other troubled individuals. Members of the community restored and maintain the buildings and grounds. They provide for their own support through earnings from their highly acclaimed service of lunches and dinners, and from items that they make and sell in their gift shop. Everything about their lives, as well as the buildings and grounds, radiates the significance and power of community.

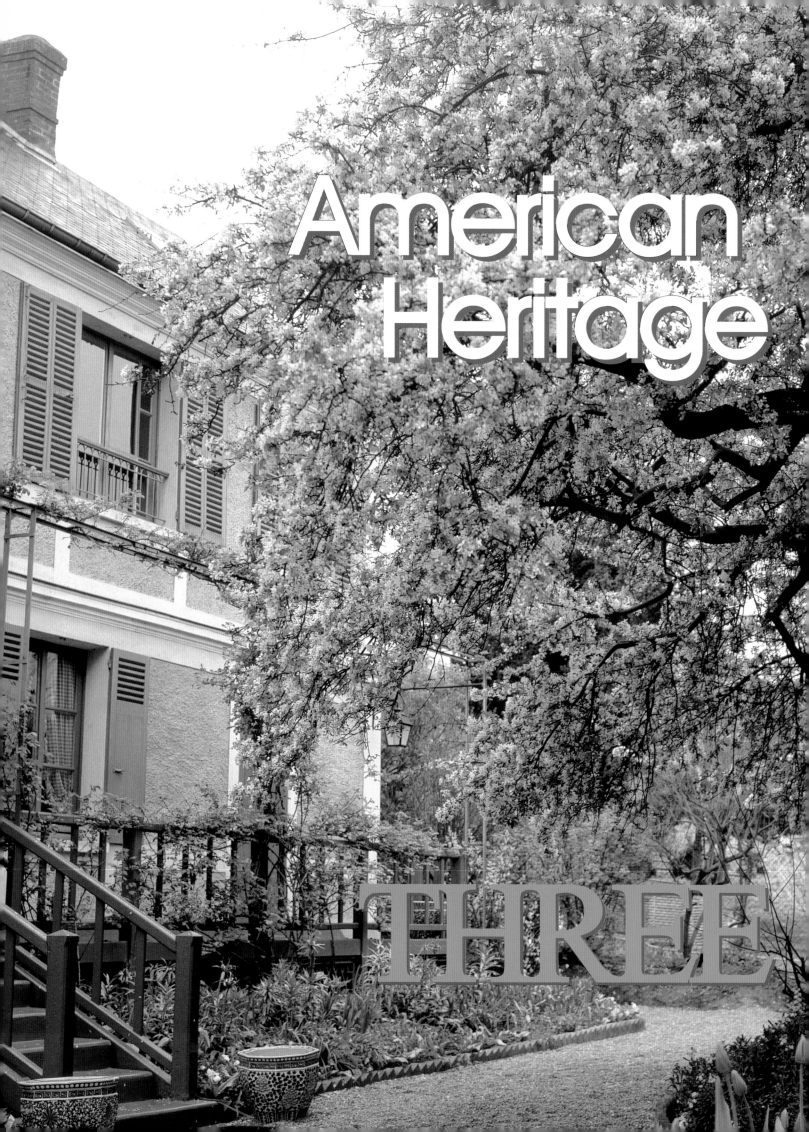

American Heritage

THREE

*"Individual liberty is individual power,
and as the power of a
community is a mass compounded of
individual powers, the nation
which enjoys the most freedom must necessarily
be in proportion to its numbers the
most powerful nation."*

– John Quincy Adams

A Nation of Dreams

The United States is a relatively young country, and to this day retains certain intimations of the "New World," that idea so attractive to the money, manpower and imagination of Europe during its colonizing era. Indeed, America began both as colony—a subset of British society and tradition—and frontier, a wild place, utterly without precedent. The sheer size of the country and diversity of its physical landscape, the challenge and hardship of newness, and the inevitable conflict between tradition and innovation were the early forces that shaped today's particularly American ideas about community.

On the Eastern Seaboard, both the physical and social structures of English towns were modified to afford necessary protections against the wilderness, the elements and Native American tribes. Western pioneers borrowed what they could from Eastern cities, as well as from the architecture of the earlier Spanish explorers and missionaries, but took these items a step further, modifying them again and again to create a workable community structure in a hostile landscape.

Nothing it created in the New World ended up quite as it started out to be; no imitation was the same as the original in form or function. Translated across an ocean or an expanse of continent, stylistic traditions, materials and uses morphed into something new and different. What resulted was nothing less than the icons of American community life that we view today as timeless and even monolithic. Yet they began as a borrowing of ideas that traveled from Europe to New England to the Southern colonies to the Western frontier and back again, at each stop picking up some new addition, dropping some old function, finding a new name or a new use.

The spirit of a people in the process of becoming; this is our heritage and the true American dream. An adventurous spirit and willingness to explore are just as crucial at the planning tables and computer screens of today as in the forests and fields of our earliest beginnings. And if we choose, these accomplishments of long ago can be used as a springboard for the continuous creation of something new as our contribution to the future.

Learning From New England

The towns, cities, fields, forests and roads of New England virtually sing with tradition and history. The collection of states that make up this distinctive region of America share a legacy of being some of the earliest British colonies. However, while names such as Cambridge, Oxford, New Haven and New London evoke the venerable old centers of the Old World, New England is primarily distinguished as the birthplace of the new America—of its ideals, politics and laws. Here is where the Boston Tea Party took place, where the Declaration of Independence was conceived, where Paul Revere rode to warn against the Redcoats, where "no taxation without representation" was raised as a battle cry, and where our "founding fathers" lived and died.

New England, then, is something of a community writ large, sharing perhaps the strongest historic legacy and cultural landscape of any place in this country. As we have seen, such ties to the past can present a great challenge to creating artful, dynamic and forward-looking community in the here and now. New England's success, however, has been its insistence on building bridges *between* past and present. The richness of tradition has been enlisted into the service of artful community for today—and tomorrow.

New England shines with history but has examples as fresh and innovative as the best custom-designed communities of today. New England is a particular place with a special history and legacy, but the obvious care that has gone into what we admire most is not something bound by place. Styles of architecture, distinctive physical landscapes or cultural histories may—and should—vary from place to place. Yet the *soul* of community, those principles of artfulness that are not bound by land forms and go much deeper than style, can—and should—be transferred from place to place.

An American Icon

A colorful, busy Main Street and a venerable, tree-lined Elm Street; a wide civic boulevard with stately white buildings rising at either end; a town square and a hardwood-floored meeting house; a "city beautiful," complete with heroic skyscrapers and fantastic new architectural design; a neatly manicured urban park and landscaped garden; a railroad, ranging across the plains carrying gritty and precious cargo, and then the raucous port city where it will stop to unload...

Even brief descriptions of these places ring warm and familiar in our ears. In all their diversity, each resonates with the same comfort and quiet joy: a shared heritage, a timeless story, sepia-toned and sacred. These feelings are the stock in the soup of our dream of community. And yet when we sit down to plan, to untangle the gnarled problem of sprawl, to rezone or debate the future of our town or city, our language is parched, our imaginations stymied and our conversation bickering. We seem to believe the language of dream, of shared memory, is off the table. Until we open our dialogue to the richness of what we feel, we will continue to plan with the least of ourselves, instead of the greatness of our spirit and heritage.

Camden, Maine: *Camden's Public Library first opened its doors on June 1, 1928. The land was donated by a private citizen, and resident fundraisers were held to cover the cost of construction. Nearly a half century later, citizens and businesses banded together again to build a major addition. Rather than just adding the needed space, the new plan was mindful of the scenic and historic character of the original library and its setting. The result was to build a substantial portion of the addition below grade, preserving the expansive grass area shown above. With connecting gardens, including one especially for children, the library now serves as a cultural and intellectual center for the greater community.*

Dynamic Regeneration: *The houses to the right were once new. They lived out their useful life, aged and momentarily died, but they will be new again. The office buildings above and the seaside buildings on the facing page all went through the same process of birth, death and renewal, and in their new lives they also have new functions. This in microcosm is what takes place in the growth and transformation of all human settlements, and every time a change takes place, it is an opportunity to improve on the past.*

82

The Cycle of Life: *For the most part, new communities have yet to understand that real towns have cemeteries. To acknowledge that our heritage includes both yesterday and tomorrow is simply to recognize that life is best when it includes a more rooted sense of community. While there is much that is seductive about escape, to run from any part of the human experience is to run from life.*

Colonial Williamsburg

Once Great Britain's largest American colony, this 18th-century Virginia capital was anchored on one end by the seat of government and on the other by the College of William and Mary.

In terms of community, what Williamsburg symbolizes best is an idea whose time should come again. In the original town plan there was no difference in architectural character between, for example, the taverns and their neighboring houses. All were places of both life and work, complete with gardens and shops. Williamsburg's mix of uses represented the total industry of the time, including forges, silversmiths, printers, bookbinders, cabinet-makers, apothecaries, weavers, millineries, candle and soap shops, bakers and bootmakers.

Now fast-forward to the 21st century, where municipal ordinances demanding separation of land uses are exceeded only by the private sector's more stringent covenants, conditions and restrictions that memorialize the separation of life and work into perpetuity. While separation may be justified to preclude the imposition of incompatible activities, it also precludes complimentary relationships, which could conserve energy, reduce congestion and add vitality where our current patterns of separation have produced a numbing sameness.

Chautauqua, New York

Chautauqua is a 225-acre, gated, 130-year-old, educational, cultural, recreational and religious settlement located within a beautifully wooded lake setting in western New York. The entire community is a National Historic District. A guiding philosophy provides for the stewardship of its timeless heritage, while continually reaching out for the emerging insights in all areas of human endeavor.

A Model for the Future

Beyond its significance as an historic treasure, Chautauqua is a living presence that has provided inspiration for communities of the future, including the high-profile town of Celebration, Florida. Architects, planners and developers continue to visit Chautauqua to learn its lessons as they continue their own pursuit of community in ever new and uncharted ways.

Like its many-themed community followers, Chautauqua is both picturesque and quaint, but it also is far more. Developments that are heavily themed are almost always expressions of the past. By contrast, Chautauqua began in the distant past but is all about the future. Because they are mainly restatements, themed developments tend to be fixed in time. Because Chautauqua is an original, it exists in a living state of exploration and change.

Chautauqua's physical character can be seen as everything from a city in miniature to an idealized country village with a culture that reflects the American spirit at its highest and most comprehensive level of commitment. In J.H. Vincent's, *Chautauqua Movement,* he describes the early days as "a two-week session of lectures, normal lessons, sermons, devotional meetings, conferences and illustrative exercises, with recreative features in concerts, fireworks, and one or two humorous lectures."

He goes on to describe Chautauqua as a "protracted institute held in the woods." Nearly a century and a half later, its original passion and ideals can be felt in many ways, for example in its grouping of cottages in direct proximity to the community's amphitheater. Rather than separation, this central gathering place symbolizes the citizen involvement of the Chautauqua idea. In providing the setting for ongoing performances of all kinds, the amphitheater serves as the very heart of the community.

Guided by Philosophy

Werner Heisenberg, the celebrated physicist, demonstrated that the mere act of measuring alters the measurements. The way we have evaluated proposals for land use in the past has favored the clarity of sameness, because it is easier to measure. This has produced monotony and separation. Chautauqua has its own 42-page set of architectural and land-use rules that regulate everything from "bulk, proportion and scale" to "windows, doors, porches and hot tubs." The difference is that Chautauqua's place in history has little to do with its measurable details and everything to do with its commitment to the philosophic values of community. What is so deeply felt in the Chautauqua environment is the inspiration of its spiritual essence. In designing communities for the future, there is much that can be learned from the six bulleted excerpts on the facing page which are paraphrased from Chautauqua's "Statement of Philosophy."

- Buildings representing a folk interpretation of contemporaneous popular styles. These are more important in the aggregate than as individual structures.

- An idealized country village—in essence, a city in miniature.

- Pedestrian boulevards that meander through acres of trees.

- Open-air public buildings, living life in public spaces and on open porches as much as inside one's home.

- A celebration of heritage and urban design.

- A community planned to accommodate people in the pursuit of spiritual and intellectual betterment.

"...It has its own mythic force, Chautauqua does. And while there have been other chautauquas so called, this is <u>the</u> Chautauqua. There is no place like it. No resort. No spa. Not anywhere else in the country, or anywhere else in the world. It is at once a summer encampment and a small town—a college campus, an arts colony, a music festival, a religious retreat and a village square. It is all of these, and none of these, just..."

– David McCullough

Chautauqua is far more than its own special place. It stands as inspiration for the power and permanence of ideas over the fits and starts of circumstance that can seem so compelling in our decision-making at the time. It represents the highest triumph of community planning and stewardship—which is for the life it supports to be enhanced by the physical environments created for that purpose.

The Early Days: *To the right is the Chautauqua amphitheater, sometime before 1876, and the 1879 master plan for the overall grounds.*

Conservation, Change and Renewal

Where community exists, people tend to do the right things for holistic reasons rather than by way of disjointed crusades. It is more difficult and far less rewarding to restore a treasured but isolated building than it is to care for one that exists in a nurtured context. Chautauqua's Hultquist Center for Continuing Studies provides an excellent example. It was originally built in 1889 as the Chautauquan and Assembly Herald Building. Over time, the building was used for administrative offices and then later modified to serve as a retail store before being used as a residence. Each of these uses served the community for a time.

Its original character was eventually restored to provide classrooms with exhibition and conference space to support the Institution's mission of lifelong learning and spiritual growth. The adaptive re-use restored the building's original covered porch and joined two stand-alone sections with a double-height lobby. Technology of the present was deployed in a way that didn't exist a century earlier, giving the building new life for the future while expressing reverence for its past. It exemplifies the need to bridge between what we have been given and our own commitments to give our best to those who are yet to come.

Historic Treasures: *The Miller Bell Tower (top photo) has become the symbol of Chautauqua. It was built in 1911 in honor of Lewis Miller, the Institution's co-founder. The tower's 14 bells, 10 of which were manufactured in 1885, are played three or four times a day. The largest, a 3,033-pound bell, is used to announce community events. The Athenaeum Hotel (above), built in 1881, was the first hotel in the world to have electric lighting. Nine U.S. Presidents beginning with Ulysses S. Grant have visited Chautauqua. Teddy Roosevelt, Thomas Edison, Susan B. Anthony, Duke Ellington, Marion Anderson, Robert Kennedy and former President Clinton have been among the Athenaeum's well-known guests. Sensitive renovations and additions have preserved the history of the hotel while providing for its continual use and vitality.*

Convenience, Pleasure, Inspiration:

The community tram station is located just inside Chautauqua's main gate. The middle photo above is a view toward the amphitheater, which is open to the surrounding gardens and houses. The above photo was taken inside the amphitheater, which is in constant use for everything from lectures and theatrical presentations to a wide variety of concerts. The center photos are of the open-air Hall of Philosophy, where ideas are shared, developed and celebrated. The seasonal influx of residents, performers and guests flows like lifeblood, giving ever-growing meaning to Chautauqua's presence and purpose.

Beyond "Amenities"

The community of Chautauqua is rich with what developers call "amenities," including 36 holes of golf, extensive sailing programs and a yacht club located on the community's expansive 18-mile lake frontage whose beauty is second to none. But the community's heart and soul consists of commitments and provisions that exist far beyond the reach of any easy-to-describe features. Among the greatest of these is Chautauqua's 5000-seat open-air, covered amphitheater, where spiritual, intellectual and cultural activities are presented both by day and by night. Pictured above is the Chautauqua Symphony Orchestra. When the seats behind the orchestra aren't used for a choir, they are used by fans who want to sit near their favorite section of the orchestra. The background of pipes are from the great Massey

organ, which is the oldest outdoor instrument of its kind still in operation. Chautauqua's other performing organizations include its opera, ballet, theater group and the Music School Festival Orchestra. In addition to the community's many churches, a nondenominational sacred song service is held in the Amphitheater every Sunday, and lectures are given throughout the week.

In the holistic atmosphere of Chautauqua, science, faith, reason, economics, international and national affairs, urban design, literature, dance and music are not so much studied as "subjects" as they are an intrinsic part of living with a deeper sense of inquiry and appreciation for the excitement and mysteries that enrich daily life.

Culture as a Way of Life

Many of our cherished institutions are in decline and fighting for survival. It may well be that the time has passed when symphonies, choral groups, operas, dance troops and even educational organizations can thrive as isolated venues. Chautauqua's example shows what energy can be generated when individual pursuits are empowered by an integrated community context.

Consider the difference between attending a symphony concert in a typical city or town versus attending one at Chautauqua, starting with the makeup of the audience. At Chautauqua, there are two kinds of people—those staying on the grounds and those coming from surrounding areas. As compared to a more typical city or town, the culture is one of total immersion in what the place is all about. There are as many televisions, VCRs and other distractions as anywhere else, but Tuesdays, Thursdays and Saturdays are "symphony nights." Enthusiastic attendance is more like the predictability of night following day than the need for a conscious decision.

For the attendees who live off the grounds, just coming into the Chautauqua community is part of the magnetism. In a very real sense, the performance starts before the first sound, because the community itself is an inseparable part of its offerings. Other cities and towns that have created cultural districts—especially those that include lively residential settings—attempt to achieve this same magnetism.

How about the performers? At Chautauqua, the season starts with a reception at the president's house attended by the community's administration and guests; thus the musicians feel valued. The musicians wear dark jackets, but everything else is white. Whether they live on or off the grounds, they walk. And when they walk, they are recognized by citizens who admire them for their accomplishments. When they perform, it is to a knowing audience. In any city or town where this excitement isn't present, it can produce an atmosphere that makes it seem as though neither the audience nor the musicians want to be there.

What about the physical relationship between the orchestra and the audience? At Chautauqua's open-air amphitheater there is no proscenium to cause a visual separation between the stage and seating areas. The performers and those who have come to enjoy their music are in one big space, open to and surrounded by adjacent houses. Do the people who live in these houses complain about the noise and crowds? Hardly. Their balconies become coveted box seats.

While Chautauqua is admittedly special, it is always the special case that stretches our concept of the possible. It is special places and special achievements that inspire us beyond the limits of our reasoning minds, which are always ready to explain why anything exceptional isn't possible. But for the fact that it exists, Chautauqua itself isn't possible, and so it is with anything truly worthwhile.

Unselfconscious Loveliness: *In addition to spaces programmed specifically for public use, the entire Chautauqua environment "lives" like an interconnected series of outdoor rooms to be experienced by residents and guests alike. One-, two-, three-, and four-story porches provide a felt connection between inside and outside space. Pedestrian-scaled streets, vistas to the lake and other special features, along with a designed response to topographic change, all add their own magic. Houses, large and small, single- and multi-family, exist side by side in a seamless tapestry that includes inns and shops, connected by paths and trails that lead to parks, plazas, churches and other gathering places.*

Celebration, Florida

When compared to the multi-generational evolution of Chautauqua, the development of Celebration (as shown on this and the facing page) can be studied as a more instant phenomenon. Its major first phases were programmed, planned and executed within a decade, all under the direction of a single corporate entity. That some view the result as being less "real" is not so much of an insight or criticism as it is a simple fact of the centralized power and timing of its delivery system. Founded in 1994, this Walt Disney Company-developed town represents a comprehensive expression of the neo-traditional approach patterned after the American towns of the 1920s. The initial development included a highly integrated diversity of housing types, employment, retail, and a host of public amenities, all exquisitely designed, detailed and executed.

96

Picture-Perfect: *What Celebration's developer set out to accomplish has been executed with uncommon perfection. The deliberateness of its design, development and governance provides a textbook clarity. It is the kind of clarity that will inevitably be studied over time to test its original assumptions as to what would be in the long-term interests of all present and future citizens.*

97

Charleston, South Carolina

Charleston not only inspires love at first sight, but the longer the exposure, the greater the love. It is both richly historic and vibrantly alive. Its town planning and architecture are inseparable, and its culture wears the patina of time. More than most cities, it accommodates the automobile while celebrating the pedestrian. Its narrow streets may be lined with cars, but walking remains a joy.

It is not surprising that Charleston has inspired a host of imitators. When poorly done, the copies appear eerily strange, like people in period dress, perfect for a costume party but highly peculiar for everyday life. When done well, development inspired by the original can be executed at such a high level that it transcends imitation to stand on its own as more of a good thing. While Charleston's lessons are many, they will never replace the need for each generation to think for itself.

Walking and Driving

One Christmas, I had the pleasure of attending a black-tie dinner in Charleston's historic South of Broad section. When it came time for the 30 or so guests to leave, being from the Southwest, I was shocked to realize that many people simply walked to their homes. Everything about Charleston's urban setting is conducive to walking, including smaller lots with two- and three-story houses and sidewalks embraced by ornamentally fenced and raised yards on one side and tree-lined streets with parallel parking on the other.

But unlike the unfounded claims made for the Charleston look-alikes, what this pedestrian atmosphere didn't do was reduce the number of cars. It didn't take much for me to learn that every person of driving age had his or her own car and that the number of annual miles driven was about the same as for those living in conventional suburbia.

The Corner Store

I was a house guest where the party occurred the night before. The following morning, I accompanied my host on a lovely three-minute walk to Mr. Burbage's market, a dream of a place for anyone who longs for the charm of the past. The white-frame building occupies a corner site and fits in as though it were just another house. The shop has operated in the same family for more than a half century. This continuity has resulted in a loyal following from an equally stable base of local residents.

A Town Planner's Dream: *Mr. Burbage, standing in front of his neighborhood market, is an image of service, charm and personal care, all within walking distance of customers he knows by name.*

Because Mr. Burbage's volume is low, all the prices are a little higher and there are many items for which he can't compete at any price—fresh vegetables, for example. So all who shop with Mr. Burbage also use their cars to shop in more conventional suburban locations, where they make the majority of their purchases.

Corner Stores of the Future

Tomorrow's "corner store" will combine the personal, long-term commitment of a Mr. Burbage with the management savvy of a big-box retailer and the global inventory of a gourmet superstore. Its "feel" will be more residential than commercial and ideally located to serve its repeat customers, most of whom will be called by name.

These one-of-a-kind places are part of a greater story. They are the catalysts for injecting new life and value into the accumulated 50 years of suburban development that is now ripe for renewal. To take advantage of this opportunity will require changing our governing codes and ordinances to provide for the complexities of mixing land uses, densities, building heights and, where appropriate, reduced parking requirements. The whole process of jurisdictional review must be made to encourage creativity in everything from overall planning to the smallest details of signage, color and lighting. When we make our codes and ordinances the servants of human values rather than the other way around, our pent-up desire for the joy of community will do the rest. This new direction is further discussed and illustrated on pages 121 to 127.

Three Steps in the Right Direction: *Top photo: La Grande Orange, a true neighborhood market and gathering place in Phoenix, Arizona. Middle: EatZi's, a gourmet superstore in Dallas, Texas. Bottom: a Wal-Mart, richly designed and landscaped, including underground parking, in Merida, Mexico. Each of these examples contributes to its community purpose and setting by way of creative design. These three scales of the new marketplace are part of the search for ways to combine the human experience of the "mom-and-pop" shops of yesterday with the far greater demands and opportunities of the 21st century.*

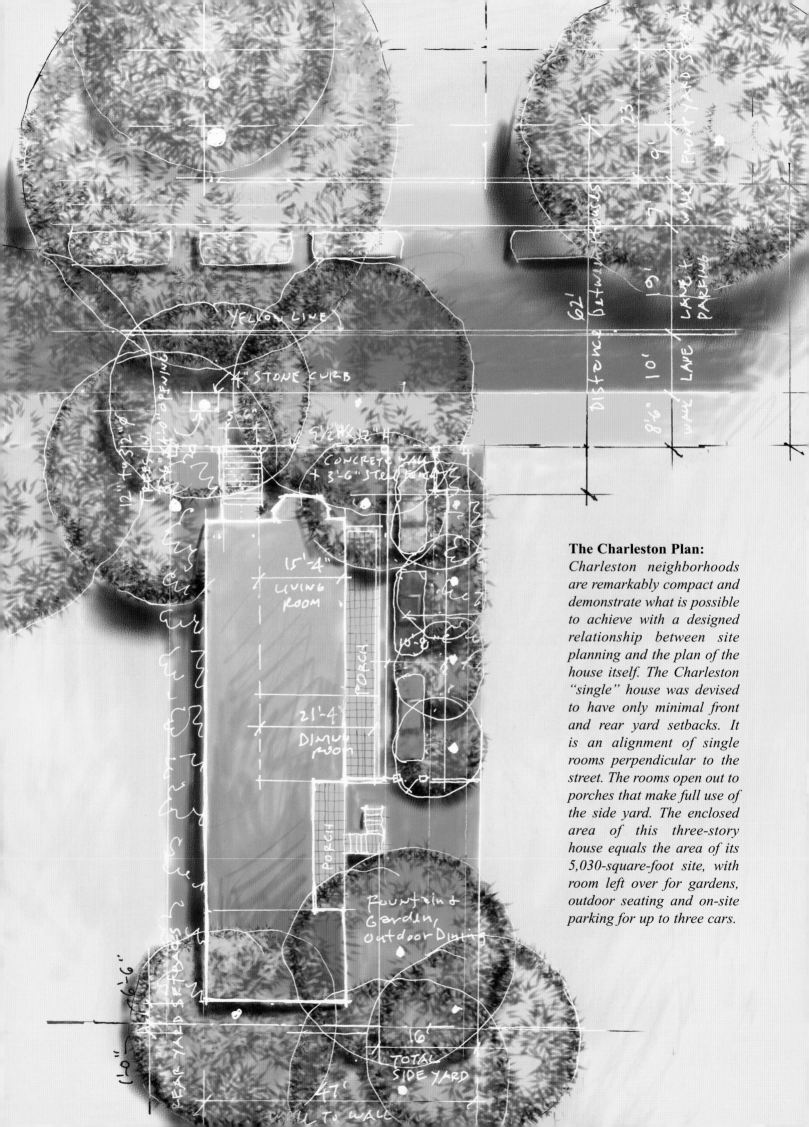

The Charleston Plan:
Charleston neighborhoods are remarkably compact and demonstrate what is possible to achieve with a designed relationship between site planning and the plan of the house itself. The Charleston "single" house was devised to have only minimal front and rear yard setbacks. It is an alignment of single rooms perpendicular to the street. The rooms open out to porches that make full use of the side yard. The enclosed area of this three-story house equals the area of its 5,030-square-foot site, with room left over for gardens, outdoor seating and on-site parking for up to three cars.

Genuine Diversity: *The top two photos of houses on Charleston's Battery district are living testimony to the magic of authentic design. They appear as related as if they were conceived as a single composition, yet each home is different in form, materials, height, detailing and massing. Gated courtyards and indoor/outdoor living areas afford individuality and charm. The middle photos are of Charleston's famed Rainbow Row.*

More of a Good Thing

If the historic Charleston single house and its related site planning work so well, why not simply reproduce both in new development? That is exactly what some are doing. The images on this page are of historic Charleston, including the top photo of houses surrounding Colonial Lake. The images on the facing and two following pages are of I'On, a new community in nearby Mount Pleasant. Unlike the spread of development around historic Charleston that repeats the patterns of suburbia everywhere, I'On is an extension of the character and diversity of the original.

I'On's six neighborhoods are each arranged around some form of open public park, square or lake. The architecture reflects South Carolina's classic Low Country vernacular. The community's exemplary execution is testimony to the strength and commitment of its developers. But not even the promise of such excellence was sufficient to stop the approval process from taking its toll. What would have been a more workable amount and mix of commercial uses was reduced, and the proposed inclusion of apartments and "granny flats" that would have permitted a greater integration of income groups was not allowed.

Exploratory Integration

FOUR

"The campus ... offers a vibrant mix of public and private spaces, linked by pedestrian routes. Housing, work, shopping and recreation are all quickly and easily accessible... It puts a variety of functions within reach of pedestrians (while offering other transportation choices as well); it offers housing for people of different incomes and lifestyles, from single-parent to classic family to elderly; and it restores public life by creating streets and plazas where people can gather comfortably."

– Diane Dulken

The Campus as Community

Anyone who has attended college has experienced what it means to be part of a true live/work community. The college campus is designed with unusual intentionality. Buildings and landscape blend together in support of learning and working.

Almost all campus spaces are multi-use. Classrooms serve as meeting spaces for clubs, organizations and special events; dormitory common rooms are used for study by day and social gathering by night; rolling green lawns are variously taken over for athletic practice, spontaneous picnicking, sunbathing, study groups or public campus tours.

Many colleges offer work-study programs, allowing students to man their own libraries, work their own kitchens or serve as departmental research assistants for their professors. These programs are popular not only because they help defray tuition costs, but because they offer a concrete way to make a contribution to the community. Residential dormitories are headed up by elected student officials and are organized to foster community,

diversity and expertise in cooperation and conflict resolution. College towns are known for their particular vibrancy, their plethora of restaurants, clubs, and other entertainment venues, the quality of their public grammar schools and high schools, and their focus on the arts, culture and learning. Campus athletic facilities, gardens, paths and lawns are generally open to the larger public, creating a place of connection that enhances both student and town life.

This living, working, playing, learning and meeting all takes place within the exceptional beauty that tends to characterize campus environments. Such campuses are often the crown jewel in a well-known planner's portfolio, and high-level firms have traditionally competed to design additional buildings. Trustees defend the landscape with utmost sincerity and rigor, screening new projects to ensure the integrity of the original intent. Alumni contribute year after year to the upkeep of this legacy, desiring to maintain the beauty they remember as being so central to their experience.

University of Illinois at Urbana-Champaign

Artful Design: *College campuses from coast to coast provide an indelible lesson that so many intuitively understand. At the intersection of life, work and learning, we must have beauty. Because the campus is a place of special function, we take care to shape it artfully, creating beauty that appeals to our highest natures, employing design that will last through the generations. The challenge before us is to bring this care into the design of the everyday, all in pursuit of the artful community and, ultimately, artful world.*

University of South Florida, Tampa

University of San Diego

Another Reality

People often dismiss college towns as "not the real world," as cushy and sequestered places that keep the harsh realities of adult life at bay. Inasmuch as we desire artfulness in our lives and our dwelling places, the college campus can be seen as a model to be emulated. The differences between college and post-college years are obvious; students do not work 40-hour weeks to pay bills, and they often live in busy dormitories instead of single apartments. However, to discount the college experience as something separate from real life tends to prevent us from learning its far more important lessons.

It is time we stopped deeming artfulness to be somehow less real or important than the artlessness of daily life. The solution is not to bring the "real world"—including congestion and sprawl—into the campus, but to bring the artfulness of the campus off the hill and into the world. Styles of architecture and landscaping vary widely from campus to campus, but in each can be found the elements of a creative live/work community, and a beauty designed to enhance the life within.

The most important lesson to be drawn from campus settings is the power and cohesiveness that comes about with intention. In other words, their physical environments express a coherent idea. This distinctive character has also been achieved by our most admired cities and towns. Conversely, it is suburbia's lack of any coherent sense that is its most obvious flaw.

Smith College

Designed as an arboretum by Frederick Law Olmsted, Smith maintains renowned botanic gardens, rare species of trees and spectacular walking paths. Thanks to its manageable size and particular beauty, the campus is something of a public park that serves members of the surrounding community. One is as likely to run into a "townie" enjoying the campus as a student walking to class. Smith's gardens are working laboratories for botany and science students, and contribute specimens to regional hospitals and research institutions. Frequent and famous "bulb shows" attract crowds from New England and beyond, welcoming the public to enjoy the artfulness of Olmsted's historic design. Paradise Pond, shown to the right, is surrounded on all sides by athletic fields, trails and a teahouse, all in view of the botanic gardens and greenhouse. This area of the campus is the main point of connection between the college and the surrounding community. A car-accessible drive and gate open out onto one of the main town streets, inviting everyone to enjoy the grounds. The design provides a sense of wide-open space with a multiplicity of things to do, all close at hand. Boating, swimming, exercising, gardening, research and outdoor study are among the daily activities for the students and community. For the college, the Paradise Pond area is a second center of the campus, away from the academic buildings but as heavily trafficked. Equally important, it is a well-loved resource, a recreational area and meeting place for the greater community.

A Quiet Place: *This terraced courtyard in the middle of Smith's performing-arts complex connects a music library, rehearsal studios, the lobby of the main theater and the music recital hall. The terraces and wide stone benches that occur beneath flowering trees are perfectly suited to gentle recreations of the mind: writing, reading, study, intimate conversation, painting or drawing, and meditation. In the evenings, the Northampton community frequents this cozy courtyard for pre-theater gatherings, cookouts, outdoor dance recitals, fencing exhibitions and small farmers' markets.*

The Quadrangle at Smith College

The Northampton Renaissance

Not more than 15 years ago, Northampton, Massachusetts, the town that hosts Smith College, was failing and dilapidated. Once a busy mill town and port along the Connecticut River, it had been in decline since World War II, its only draw being the affluent "college on the hill." Believing this perceived separation to be a waste of potential, Smith approached the then mayor of Northampton with resources and a plan for the revival of the downtown area. Working together, the college and the community in-filled compact and beautifully landscaped parks, restored historic building façades, rezoned several streets to encourage the proliferation of "mom-and-pop" shops, and overhauled and re-opened various small museums of local history. Today, Northampton is listed by *Urban Land Magazine* as one of the "10 best-preserved unique communities in America." It is the subject of a best-selling book, *Hometown*, by Pulitzer Prize-winning author Tracy Kidder; it is the thriving center of the region's arts and music scene, home to well-restored and famous theaters and venues that have won the respect of even the most cutting-edge music critics; and it is one of the prime destinations for families vacationing in New England, discriminating antique hunters, young hipsters, regional small businesses looking for a sure market for all kinds of goods and services, and more. This turnabout, a renaissance in the truest sense, would not have been possible without the shared belief that both town and college would be seriously diminished without the other.

Hampshire College

Hampshire is the newest addition to what is now the Five College Consortium of Smith, Mount Holyoke, Amherst and the University of Massachusett at Amherst. The consortium can be seen as a regional community comprised of both towns and institutions, each unique in its own identity but enhanced by shared characteristics not bound by property lines or village limits. Students enjoy greater resources as well as the feeling that comes from belonging to a multifaceted community. As for the surrounding college towns, the constortium is a shared source of pride and a resource for all, including free buses that run all day every day, connecting the colleges and towns for both students and the surrounding citizenry.

Smith and Hampshire make excellent examples of the campus as community, because that is the essence of what they have in common. In terms of physical appearance, they couldn't be more different. One of Hampshire's primary goals is to challenge the institutional hierarchies inherent in traditional education, those that place barriers between teacher and student, classroom learning and life. Hampshire's built environment was designed for a diversity of uses. The physical infrastructure supports an alternative program in which students design their own majors and fix their own graduation dates. The faculty have offices and classes in the residential dormitories, and the dorms themselves are all cooperatives.

School Days Forever

Long before the 76 million baby boomers born between 1946 and 1964 reach their sixth decade, what we now think of as "retirement" age will have blossomed into a new vitality largely centered in a rediscovered sense of community. So-called senior citizens are already the fastest growing segment of our population, with various services for the elderly having doubled and tripled in recent years. The retirement home is one such service, an institution devoted entirely to this growing demographic and bursting with potential for more integrated provisions to serve a guaranteed market that within the next three decades will become the single largest age group ever measured.

To long for retirement is understandable, especially if work is divorced from one's interests or is backbreaking or even life-threatening. A century ago, this was a pretty accurate description for most workers, nearly all of whom were men, and dying on the job was not uncommon. But what happens when work becomes inseparable from who we are? Dramatic examples of work as life are everywhere, with some of the most notable being writers, orchestra conductors, teachers, scientists and artists of all kinds.

What if we not only built things for a living but also loved building, would we ever stop pursuing our craft? What if we were not only teachers but we loved learning, would we ever stop seeking to learn? What if we were not only musicians but also loved music, would we ever stop practicing? Someone asked the great cellist Pablo Casals, then in his nineties, why he continued to practice. He answered by saying, "I think I am getting better." In his 89th year, Frank Lloyd Wright said, "One of the things I like most about myself is that I can still learn something." The sentiment is now echoing through the retirement programs of colleges and universities. There are many reasons for this new alliance, not the least of which is that medical research points to mental exercise having anti-aging benefits for the mind, just as physical exercise does for the body.

Lasell College provides one example of a movement that is being explored in greatly varying ways all over the world. The college is located in a residential suburb of Boston, complete with a 13-acre village that includes everything from independent apartments to facilities with full nursing care. The village challenges people to think of retirement in a new way, as a time for active, enriched living augmented by luxurious hospitality and opportunities for ongoing learning.

"Not only does education continue when schooling ends, but it is not confined to what may be studied in adult education courses. The world is an incomparable classroom, and life is a memorable teacher for those who aren't afraid of her."

– John W. Gardner

A Place to Grow: *Presbyterian Homes operates continued-care retirement communities that serve adults at all stages of independence and health. These images are of campuses in Evanston, Lake Forest and Arlington Heights, Illinois. These campuses provide single homes and apartments with paths, gardens and central green spaces. Common areas include dining rooms, banks, laundries and delis. Five campuses in the Chicago area are designed to have the residents relate to a more expansive community, while enjoying the intimacy of their own homes. Residents can visit the other campuses as well as go shopping, attend concerts, plays and other events, all by way of a free shuttle service. Rolling green spaces and gardens serve as parks and play spaces for adults, children and everyone in between.*

"May you live all the days of your life."
– Jonathan Swift

To acknowledge that our desire for privacy and our need for community are interdependent is a powerfully liberating idea. The highest quality of privacy is to be able to tell someone you care for that you want to be alone. It is the ability to retreat from "something." To retreat from "nothing" is not privacy, but isolation. And the more that "something" can involve the stimulation of diversity, contribution and commitment, the more possible it will be to live fully for all the years of one's life.

History and Beauty: *The Parker Ridge Retirement Community in Blue Hill, Maine integrates the cultural and physical history of the unique region where it is a beautiful feature. The greatest variable for successful communities of all kinds is the provision for interdependence between humans and the environment, between the programmatic and the inspirational, including the kind of stimulation that can only occur with the benefit of different age groups. Nowhere is this more important than in getting beyond the isolation of nursing homes that seem designed as the "last outpost" for individuals no longer able to take care of themselves physically or mentally. As much as circumstances permit, whatever form the new generation of assisted-care facilities may take, the objective will be to foster an engaged lifestyle at all ages and stages of life and health.*

119

Integrating Age Groups

To design for community engagement is to create proximities that make unplanned and uncommon encounters possible. The three-building compound shown to the right represents the new generation of multi-use facilities designed to integrate life and work. It is an artist's studio, located in the same town as the Parker Ridge Retirement Community shown on the preceding pages. Suppose that retirement communities could be expanded to include a nurturing environment for all age groups. And that they were connected by gardens, paths and trails to a perimeter of live/work compounds. By way of this safe and pedestrian-friendly precinct we could re-create the opportunity for multi-generational nurturing on a community level that was once the norm. Only this time it would occur by choice rather than being the inevitable consequence of our earlier, less mobile family structure.

The physical design of such communities wouldn't mandate any preconceived relationships, it would simply make it possible to have more convenient contact. Human need and desire would do the rest. More than one young person has acknowledged the convenience available to adults in various forms of assisted living. Similarly, many adults would love to be around children. Take a child into the halls of an assisted-living facility and watch the life come back into the residents' faces. The mutual benefits are too obvious to ignore. There are many ways to design for peace and quiet without the sensory deprivation of age-group separation.

Retrofitting Suburbia

We are nearing the time for a convergence between the experience gained in developing large-scale, new communities and the opportunity to redevelop the original suburban communities that are now in need of renewal. This will not only be a time of rebuilding structures but discovering exciting new uses far beyond that of the original dwellings.

Home as Community

The new focus will be on extending the idea of "home" to include the custom and varied provisions of community. The future will be a time of achieving what developers of the past believed impossible. The patterns of the future are already evident in the behavior of the present.

We take advantage of home deliveries, the Internet and have goods shipped by United Parcel and Federal Express. Many people love their work, and if they could figure out how to do so, would choose to avoid the kind of retirement that results in total withdrawal from their non-home life. We share a growing interest in lifelong learning, and we go to huge discount stores to stock up on provisions that are so predictably needed, there is no reason why they shouldn't be routinely delivered to our door, just the way natural gas, water, electricity and pay-per-view TV are. We no longer associate work with drudgery or factories with something that belongs on the other side of the tracks. Even heavy industry has cleaned up its act and acquired a certain cachet. An article in *The New York Times* announced that production of the Rolls-Royce has moved from "a decidedly unglamorous red-brick factory in industrial northwest England" to its new factory, "on the estate of the Earl of March at Goodwood in an area of honey-colored stone houses and gently rolling downs. A prominent architect, Sir Nicholas Grimshaw, designed the partly sub-terranean plant to blend into the countryside."

Moving Up the Economic Scale

Few boat owners either can or would want to build their own marinas, so they join a yacht club. Corporations and individuals buy fractional ownership in jet aircraft. Many people join country clubs to take advantage of shared recreation, shared kitchens and dining rooms. Because we are time-poor, we utilize daycare for our children, we hire people to maintain our houses, gardens and pools, and hardly anyone exists who hasn't at one time or another needed to rent a car. Increasing numbers of us move into planned communities where, for our own self-interests, we voluntarily submit to the complexity of design review and homeowner associations.

Work as Life

On a more personal scale, specialty workers have always gravitated toward special environments. While this has always been true, it has only now created a more mainstream market, as described in the June 2002 issue of *Urban Land*. This untapped market combines "elements of an urban loft, an incubator business office, and a single-room occupancy apartment hotel." The article goes on to describe the tenants of such facilities as including "printmakers, musicians, sculptors, glassblowers, an auto-broker, a metal fabricator and a computer graphic designer." Many places offer spaces that can be customized and personalized by each tenant. What is most interesting about the tenant mix is that such people are likely to see their work and life as being one and the same. Journalist Robert J. Samuelson characterizes this new integration of life and work by observing that "our jobs aren't what they used to be and the boundaries between labor and leisure are eroding … work has become less manual and more mental, less regimented and more collaborative, and—as an activity—less economic and more social."

This integration of life and work will require a greater variety of housing types. Adults will be more able and likely to live in the same neighborhood as their children. The result will be built-in babysitting and other good things families do to help each other. The advantages aren't limited to families. Parents with young children need help that many teenagers would love to provide.

No matter how much we cherish our privacy, we also need to be with other people. In addition to the beauty of our homes, we wish for luxury and beauty in all that surrounds what we personally own; and we wish that the community environment could be more "custom" than what developments of the past have afforded. We take vacations to visit for only brief periods of time landscapes and structures that lift our spirits. We enjoy seeing communities that are full of life. And most of all, we love to visit places that work well for those who live there and are fully engaged and alive.

We travel to distant places to attend music and theater festivals, or to see woodworkers, lace weavers, glassblowers, potters, painters, dancers and sculptors at work. Hobbies of every kind are about working at things we love to do, and most hobbies require some form of setting that communities can provide. I know of a gifted woodworker in a retirement home who requested permission to build a woodworking shop at his own expense, just so he could continue experiencing the joy of his craft.

Expanded Mobility

While we have never strayed far from our love affair with the automobile, there are elements of vehicle ownership that none of us would miss. Taking a car to be serviced is always a hassle, as is having to choose between that sports car we would love to drive and that mini-van that has carrying capacity we may only need on occasion. We can now design communities that provide for the convenient use of a variety of vehicles beyond one's primary car. Extending this provision further makes it possible to design auto-free neighborhoods without the loss of individual mobility.

For more than a decade, many European cities, including Amsterdam, Berlin and Zurich, have been developing programs that provide a variety of vehicles to individuals without the greater costs and maintenance hassles of ownership. Similar programs have sprung up from Boston and Washington D.C. to Seattle, Portland and San Francisco. There are multiple considerations that make this a winning arrangement for both the individual and the environment.

As we seek to balance the benefits of our homes with that of the surrounding community, there exists a wealth of opportunities for a blend between the two. The home of the future will be a celebration of individuality, amenities and variety, all beyond anything that exists today. For most of the 20th century, notions concerning the house of the future referred to new materials or breakthrough technologies, including robotic and computerization, that would make houses "smart" enough to reduce the need for us to think. The future will look back on this as a quaint, momentary fascination with notions and things that have become so integrated into our homes as to not be worth mentioning. The new focus will be on a more community-centered sense of individuality, privacy and performance.

Existing suburbia will be given new life by way of infill development and by retrofitting areas with village cores designed to provide identity and services for the surrounding neighborhoods. The drawing to the right is of a suburban site that had been planned in the conventional manner. Its custom community replacement, illustrated on the following pages, includes the same number of residences as the conventional approach but with far more diversity in both type and size. It also includes sufficient non-residential uses to create a live/work, inter-generational and cultural environment. The community's pathways exceed the length of its streets. Every resident lives within 700 feet of the community core. The path system extends beyond its own 33-acre site, providing pedestrian linkages to an elementary school, park, church and adjacent neighborhoods.

Conventional Suburbia: *This 33-acre site plan includes 110 lots. In typical suburban fashion, life is lived on a lot-by-lot basis. People come and go through the anonymity of their look-alike garage doors. Walking is discouraged, first because there is nothing to walk to, and second, because the walkways are most unpleasant, occurring at the edge of the street on one side and a lineup of garages on the other.*

Walkable Environments

The plan on the facing page includes a mixture of uses all within walking distance. Varied residences occur in close proximity to a core of professional offices, music, fitness, arts and craft studios, a coffeehouse, bakery, deli, an upper level bed and breakfast inn, and a series of smaller shops. The Internet has enabled new versions of the "mom-and-pop" shops where individuality, knowledge and personal service are once again both valued and possible.

The commissary provides basic supplies, home repair and ongoing maintenance, all handled efficiently, economically and in a very personal manner. The commissary's range of goods and services includes supplies, tool rentals, house and grounds maintenance, babysitting and catered meals. The stable is a pool of vehicles available on-call and delivered to each home, including SUVs, sedans, sports cars, mini-vans, pickup trucks and neighborhood electric vehicles, always serviced and clean. Immediately adjacent to the stable is an auto-free neighborhood. Other community amenities include pedestrian and cart paths, flower and vegetable plots, pools, sculpture gardens and neighborhood parks with daycare.

Retrofitting suburbia to include core villages is an opportunity for creating fresh expressions of the pedestrian-centered environments and multi-generational settings that existed before the demands of production-driven development took precedent over considerations for living fully at all stages of life.

During the last half century, the greatest impediment to creating community was the inability to commit to "place" as well as to each other. While most of us have experienced the challenges that easily occur within one's family and all other relationships, we also recognize the paradox that our self-interests are poorly served if we only act with our self-interest in mind. When thinking about high-performance living, there aren't many things that one can do alone. That is why we have churches, team sports, country clubs, art galleries, music groups and places where it is fun to go to work.

1	Flower garden
2	Cascades
3	Community gardens
4	Fruit trees
5	Water sculpture
6	Employment core
7	Café/deli
8	Shops
9	Park/daycare
10	Courtyard residential
11	Custom homes
12	Patio homes
13	Auto-free neighborhoods
14	Artist lofts
15	Party lawn and pavilion
16	Commissary
17	Stable
18	Fountains
19	Community pool
20	Neighborhood pools

Courtyard Plaza: *Providing both visual identity and a place for informal gatherings, the Courtyard Plaza includes professional offices and specialty shops. A convenience store is run by the commissary.*

Designed Luxuries

- Co-creative custom environments

- Homes that extend beyond the "house"

- Culture as a way of life

- Daily living in a resort atmosphere

- Optimal settings for life and work

- Lifelong engagement in the midst of creative activity

- More gardens, less paving

- Fewer vehicle burdens and more vehicle choices

- Reduced "hassle miles," more accessibility

- Personal gain through cooperation

- Living in a work of art

- More privacy, more individuality and yet more community.

127

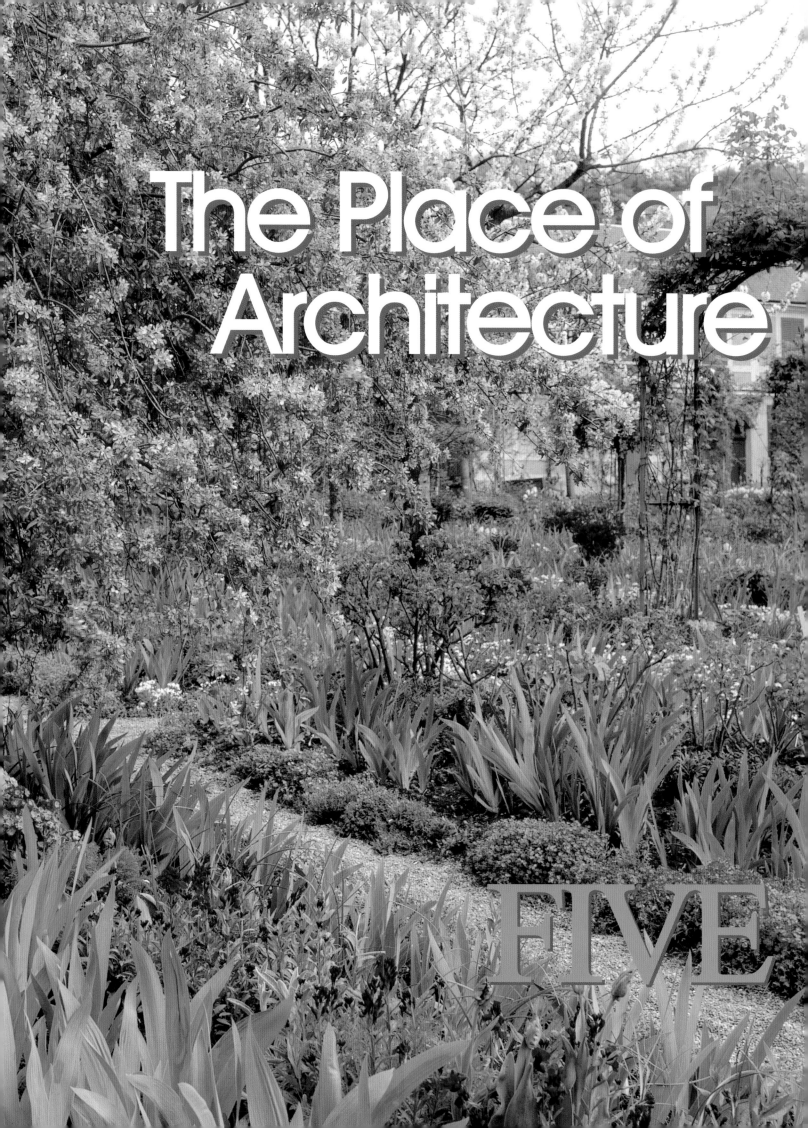

The Place of Architecture

FIVE

> *"Our architecture has been full of false starts and unfulfilled promises ... If we are to have a fine architecture, we must begin at the other end from that where our sumptuously illustrated magazines on home-building and architecture begin—not with the building itself, but with the whole complex out of which architect, builder and patron spring, and into which the finished building, whether it be a cottage or a skyscraper, is set."*
>
> – Lewis Mumford

Varieties of Practice

Unless one simply decides to avoid all such thoughts, to be an architect is to become immersed in a never-ending and daunting search for the ultimate objectives of design. Rather than be troubled by this uncertainty, I have always found it to be the wellspring for new insights. My own thoughts range from comparing the differences between one architectural practice and another, to thinking that all of humanity is in the same "business," that of making the world a better place.

If commonly held beliefs about design were categorized in terms of religion, there would be everything from fundamentalists to Unitarians, as well as those who just make it up as they go along. Like religion, no one can speak of good design without it being an expression of his underlying beliefs and assumptions, including those we accept without examination.

One of my clearest encounters with assumptions ruling design occurred in the early 1970s, during an intensive period of designing low-cost housing for what was then the nation's largest producer of manufactured mobile, modular and panelized houses. I had authored a publication for the Wisconsin Department of Natural Resources entitled *Production Dwellings, An Opportunity for Excellence.* Following its widespread publicity, the booklet resulted in a major alliance between National Homes Corporation and the Frank Lloyd Wright Foundation.

This "marriage" began with a press conference at the Park Lane Hotel in New York and was followed up with television appearances and presentations at most every home show from coast to coast. The next two years were spent in prototyping new designs. During the early stages, what I would call a "good" design because it met certain architectural principles, Jim Price, the founder and CEO of National Homes would call a "weak" design, because he couldn't readily see how to run it through his existing methods and systems. The relationship became a caldron of two worlds, where what I believed to be principles of architecture had to face what he saw as the imperatives of production. The mutual benefit to each of us was to be informed and challenged by the other. In the world of architects, the diversity of practices ranges from designers who unabashedly decorate with mannerism of the past, to architects who express the refinement of classical ideas and proportions in ever-fresh ways. Still others are innovative in their use of structure, space, methods and materials. Such innovation can produce results from the merely fanciful or shocking to the profoundly magical and sublime.

Artifacts or Community

To consider the place of architecture requires defining the word in terms of its context. For example, to speak of the architecture of the Guggenheim Museum, whether referring to New York or Bilbao, is very different from thinking about the architecture of a street, neighborhood or town. In both New York and Spain, the two museums are stand-alone artifacts that pay little homage to their respective contexts, other than as backgrounds for these heroic and dynamic pieces of sculpture. Even the most ardent admirers of such buildings would not want to see them replicated. When viewed from their exteriors, it is beyond argument that they were meant to dominate their respective settings.

The individual esteem given to iconic structures is clearly focused on the role of the architect as a soloist rather than one who is creating the greater complexity and fabric of community. The venerated architect Charles W. Moore put it this way, "Our famous architects, and many not so famous, seek always the magic moment.

They innovate with each job, and with almost no experience, since we have no real way of saying how a building or a town—a place— works, and what effect it has on the people who use it." To design for community requires an entirely different focus. Often, there is no client other than a city or a developer, the majority of which tend to avoid architectural exploration. Because they see themselves as making choices on behalf of unknown masses of people, all but the most exceptional developers regard the safest approach to be anything nostalgic. This frequently leads to imitation. Rather than get involved in the rigor of creative design, the easier approach is to look around and select from what seems to be selling well.

There is another reason developers resort to imitation, and this time the fault lies strictly with the practice of architecture itself. On more than one occasion I have encountered people who fear architecture as something separate from life, a kind of indulgent exercise in showcasing whatever passing direction may be of interest to the individual or the profession at any given time. One of the worst descriptions to be applied to architecture is the word "modern," and the majority of what it describes is architecture at its worst. When the profession decided it needed to be rescued from being tied to things "modern," it came up with the eventually discredited silliness of "postmodernism." This pathetic period was nothing but an attempt to grant respectability to what would otherwise be considered crude forms of imitation, including the grafting of recognizable fragments of classical mannerisms onto otherwise boxy structures, with little or no thought for anything but the most superficial and stylistic concerns.

The momentary infatuation with borrowing mannerisms of the past was followed by what some have called the work of "blobmeisters" and "train-wreck" or "earthquaked" design. Each of these categories includes award-winning buildings that are far more notable for their curious and idiosyncratic forms than anything to do with how well they perform the purposes for which they were created.

One thing about the curious is that it is highly publishable, often being at its best as a photograph and at its worst in real life. When the simple and the genuine can seem too subtle to be celebrated, and the daring too arbitrary to stand the test of time, we can count on a postmodern revival or some other publishable notion to momentarily take center stage.

Connective Qualities

Columbus, Indiana made history with its uncommonly large collection of public buildings designed by high-profile architects. These structures were not only stand-alone artifacts, they served as a catalyst for renewing civic pride. When the citizens of Columbus are asked what makes their town special, they are as likely to talk about their parks and the expanding "people trail" that connects all elements of their community.

While the profession of architecture has long paid lip service to the jargon of "context," the results tend to be more self-centered. Rather than the publication of newsworthy "artifacts" by "name" architects, what is needed most is to master the relationships between overall coordination and cohesiveness with the individuality and dissonances required to enliven any composition, be it music or the fabric of community.

To design well for community may be architecture's most difficult task. To design an exhibitionist building only requires that the viewer be titillated, which requires nothing more than to create large-scale puzzles. At the other extreme, and equally regrettable, are the simplistic imitations that inspired one architectural critic to refer to the houses in a highly published community as a banal collection of "Hallmark card architecture."

Good community design exists beyond the measure of most architectural dialogue. It requires a willingness to work twice as hard for half the impact. What is needed most is a search for the unselfconscious qualities that can be felt in any village that has grown its own sense of folk architecture. The challenge is to recreate this feeling without resorting to imitation, for to imitate is to thwart any hope for the lasting magnetism of the genuine. When we accept that a community demands more than a collection of star-studded artifacts, and certainly demands more than being an imitative theme park, it will change how we consider and value design.

"Communities can be shaped by choice or ... by chance. We can keep accepting the kind of communities we get, or we can insist on getting the kind of communities we want."

– Richard Moe
Changing Places

Preserving, Creating, Themeing

High-volume development often occurs at the low end of commitment, where the balance between the desirable and the possible seems obvious. It is made obvious because the participants entertain so few variables. Because they "know" that nothing more creative is possible, the best they can do is make it to whatever finish line is determined by their limited interests and understanding. There never is a better way for such people, because for them, it simply doesn't exist. Fortunately for the future, there are always others whose vision and creativity include the ability to re-frame the ground rules in order to address a more personal and long-term definition of success.

There is no better example of a creative force than Frank Lloyd Wright, for whom the only constant was change. Environments which he designed for himself, starting with his home and studio in Oak Park, Illinois, then Taliesin in Wisconsin, and later Taliesin West in Arizona, were all in a continuous state of change. All three of these places are now on the National Register of Historic Places and like many of Wright's designs, all are the subject of historic documentation, restoration and preservation.

If we were to take an inventory of the built environment, it would show that what we have most of will always fall in the category of the obvious—the suburban patterns of the last 50 years being the prime example. Less frequent are the more deliberate compositions that recreate the look of an earlier time. Rarer still would be the adaptive re-use of structures and places that have a genuine heritage. And rarest of all will always be those special places that could not exist without the far more challenging commitment to the "unknowns" of exploration and the creative spirit.

To be authentic does not require genius, but it does depend on having the courage to move beyond the familiar. Nor do genuine things have to look shockingly new. More often than not, that which screams out for attention is far more curious than profound or beautiful.

Community Values

Beyond sensitivities to price and location, when home builders wrestle with what will motivate a buyer, the easiest sell is anything that can be described and sold as a highly personal advantage or experience. Examples include lavish kitchens, luxurious master bedrooms and baths, an oversized entry, high ceilings, lots of windows and, for those who can afford it, breathtaking views, with water, golf courses, mountains and city lights being the most valued.

A tougher sell are those shared elements that enrich the surrounding community—the problem being that things shared cannot be sold so easily, because they are not seen as being so obviously owned. In fact they are very much owned. The only difference is that the owned value requires that we open ourselves up to accepting a higher, more rewarding definition of what we understand to constitute our home. Examples include tree-lined streets and lighting, fountains, vehicular and pedestrian bridges designed to add charm and beauty, convenient benches and related landscaping, signage that provides more than information, garden arbors, arches or other connecting features, and informal plazas that simply occur along paths and trails, as though provided by nature with no ulterior motive. All of these provisions, and more, are the new reality for the more sophisticated developers, builders and

home buyers. But for others, anything that doesn't translate into something private is easily discredited with the standard question, "Who is going to pay for building and maintaining these niceties?" This is the eternal question of the follower. The one who was on hand to ask why anyone would want to bring the outhouse inside their home, and the same type of person who now explains how his newly designed master bathroom has dramatically increased sales.

Most of the places depicted in this book are in some way shared. They express the essence of community; they tell us not only where we are, but who we are—something very special. Such places are an extension of our homes and in a very real sense, they are our homes. No home can mean very much if all we own stops at the front door.

Public Spaces: *A gathering of people in a parking lot can make it seem like something good is happening, but that is a momentary event. The best public spaces not only provide settings for inspiring use and enjoyment, but they radiate delight and welcome even in those in-between times when no one is on hand.*

Public Benefit From Private Development:

Colors, structures, walls, spires, gates, arches, drives and gardens created for private use, can add delight to the experience of those who may only pass by on their way to elsewhere. The possibilities for drawing inspiration from beautiful settlements of the past are endless. Most have a density higher than our suburbs, and all are made up of forms more bold, varied and sensitive to the human scale. By contrast, building in the last century was dominated by high-volume production and codes that conspired toward standardization. Instead of being the victim of circumstance, the leaders of tomorrow will use these same tools to combine the efficiencies of repetition with the artful variety of customization.

136

Tight Spaces, Human Places: *If we had only to accommodate elements like those shown in these images, creating a sense of place would be easy. Instead, the 20th century was a triumph of mass marketing and large-scale production that pushed aside the kind of human places that add poetic beauty to the fabric of community. Among the challenges of the 21st century will be to find ways to make such delightful people-centered experiences more a part of our everyday lives. Qualities like these don't show up on land-use plans or even detailed site plans. They require a focus on the ultimate three-dimensional reality. And because small-scale commercial uses and pleasurable features are no longer the norm, it places a greater emphasis on being able to achieve a rich and varied sense of community within the residential setting itself. Human delight and enjoyment require places of surprise and the animation of the unexpected. The predictability of obvious repetition and boxy massing is deadly, because it can never take advantage of the play of light and shade or even the integration of landscaping. No matter what technology may one day make possible, memorable human experiences and human values will require memorable settings of human scale.*

The Paradox of Freedom and Sameness

The people who built charming places we so easily admire were no more sensitive than today's developers, they simply had no choice but to work within their limitations, which is equally true today—the difference being that their delivery system was characterized by a limited variety of mainly natural materials, an abundance of labor and a population base that couldn't easily move away every few years.

Post-World War II America produced its own delivery system, in which both natural and created materials were abundant and generally cheaper than labor. Communication no longer required proximity, thus society became more mobile. Change was more valued than permanence, and technology not only could but did move mountains, all of which added up to more centralized, large-scale and generic handling of everything from financing and land assembly to market analysis, strategy, design and production. The inevitable result was the standardization of everything from codes and ordinances, to products and places. Left to follow their path of least resistance, this produced what we now identify as sprawl. We are technologically much freer to do anything we choose, but because we have let our new tools use us, rather than the other way around, we have created an unsatisfying sameness.

Three-Dimensional Planning

In the history of place-making, whatever we admire most has resulted from a controlling influence over the outcome. Such controls have ranged from religious to dictatorial powers. Examples would include the building of the pyramids, cathedrals and grand villas. On a more individual level, the controls required work to be done with the natural materials at hand, and for workers to work *with* the land rather than overcome it.

American democracy changed all that. By proclaiming the sovereignty of the individual and generating unprecedented industrial wealth, especially following World War II, the new delivery system became a dynamic, production-driven force. Anything seemed possible, and standardization ruled the day.

Early attempts to prescribe visual controls over production-dominated development often produced sameness, evident in suburban housing tracts, shopping centers, office parks and the thematic design of franchised businesses.

Where design guidelines have been applied to residential development—including everything from modest to high-end housing—again the tendency has been toward uniformity. Places where centralized controls were employed to create deliberate variety were more likely to be specialty theme parks, notably Disneyland and its imitators. Methods for achieving variety in community can seem counter-intuitive. The most obvious thought would be that variety is best achieved in the absence of prescriptive controls. Let a whole lot of people do whatever they wish and, according to this way of thinking, the variety will be stunning. In fact, the results are disappointing. The development of sunbelt cities like Phoenix and Las Vegas has been pretty much a free-for-all, yet the most frequent criticism is that everything looks the same.

Another attempt at obvious variety occurs when developers assign the design of specific streets or neighborhoods to different architects. This too can be problematic, a little like commissioning three composers to write a symphony in order to achieve varied movements. Symphonic variety requires a clear and central idea around which noticeably different patterns can be created, and the same is true for how we develop communities. The design of a good community should radiate the sure-footedness of a great symphony, complete with its own visual melodies and rhythms—maybe even soul.

Variety that makes us feel good can never be superficial. We detect the genuine and are attracted to it, because it hints at a greater story. Variety need not be historic to be authentic, but it must be rooted in its own special source, be that traditional or creative.

We know that books don't write themselves, paintings don't just happen, and symphonies require a composer. Similarly, beautiful streets don't plan themselves and workable neighborhoods don't just happen. If we want the greater community to add up to something special, it will need to be composed.

Composing Neighborhoods

The drawings to the right represent a process that starts with a thorough analysis of the site and the programming of intended elements. Everything that follows is a balancing act between respecting environmental considerations, securing municipal approvals, providing for the opportunities and needs of those who will make the development their home, and exploring the most effective design strategies for creating a special place.

The following 12 items are chapter headings in a narrative that sets forth the character of a residential district, much the way a composer scores the creation of a symphony. Like the complexity of notations in a musical score, each item provides direction that demands all-out commitment. Taken together, they form a series of value-enhancing relationships, including form, materials, texture, color and a balance between private and community spaces. The goal is a community of sculptural "music."

- The idea and vision

- Neighborhood character

- Residential types and relationships

- Environmental site plan

- Architectural site plan

- Streetscape plans and sections

- Parks and open space

- Engineering compatibility

- Site walls and fences

- Signage and identification

- Landscape and hardscape

- Design guidelines and governance

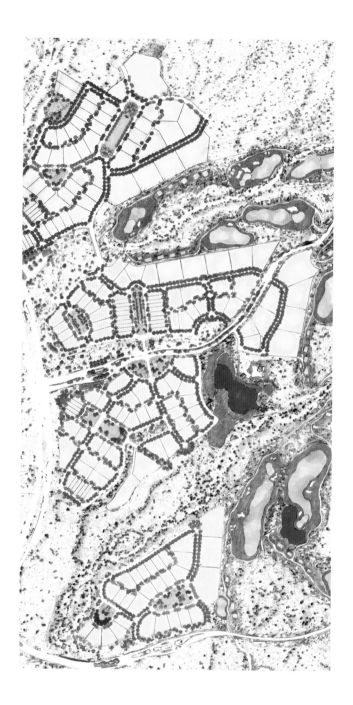

Land Use and Circulation: *Building envelopes are defined by natural drainageways, the location of valuable vegetation and the location of planned amenities. The above plan indicates a system of interconnected parks, paths and trails as well as the relationships to a golf course.*

Integrated Mix of Residences: *The color-coded plan is tied into a series of detailed designs for both standard and special conditions, including desired massing, views, garage locations and the relationships between the private and public spaces.*

Illustrated Site Plan: *This is a composite of all other design considerations. It illustrates the combined provisions of land use, trees, individual park sites and all edge conditions between developed areas and areas to be left in their natural states.*

143

Pedestrian-Scaled Streets and Parks

Beyond what can be indicated in the various kinds of plans, the "composing" process includes three-dimensional imaging to convey the more detailed provisions of the concept.

- Small parks are given prominent locations in order to become especially useful for informal play.

- Homes designed with active rooms in front overlook the street and park.

- Upper level porches treat the street as an outside room.

- Street trees create intimacy by narrowing the visual perspective.

- One-way streets increase pedestrian safety and residential character.

- A sense of privacy is provided in a short distance by front yards that step up from the sidewalk and front porches that step up from the yards.

- Sidewalks feel public because of their lower level, and safe because they are separated from the street.

- When the lots are narrow, all garages are accessed by rear lanes or alleys.

Understanding What It All Becomes: *Buildings are far more than the drawings from which they are produced, and artful communities are more than a collection of buildings. The sameness of suburbia is the result of formula-driven, desk-top planning by people who may have never walked the site. To plan with three-dimensional care not only requires intimate familiarity with the land, but the development of drawings like those on the facing page that take into account how everything will look and feel once fully developed.*

Customizing Production

The objective is to combine what is needed for efficient production with what is desirable for individuality and community. The solution has two parts. The first is to consider the site plan as a coordinated whole, treating its overall form, massing, color, special features and landscaping with as much overall control as one would give to a complex but single structure. The second is to create a kit consisting of: 1) The basic house plans and elevations;

2) Modular add-on spaces; 3) Custom homes which extend the established character of the production models into a greater variety and size; 4) Site elements, for example, pools, gazebos, towers and guest houses and; 5) Special community features, including bridges, ramadas, paths, trails, resting areas and, wherever possible, terminal vistas and focal points by way of arbors or other connecting elements.

More Than Houses: *Even for areas where there are only houses, a village quality can be achieved with the conscious use of both private and community features designed to add interest and variety to the overall sense of scale and placement of structures on the land.*

1	Custom homes	8	Pools and terraces
2	Hillside plazas	9	Office/guest house
3	Shared open space	10	Children's playhouse
4	Street plazas	11	Arrival point
5	Paths and trails	12	Entertainment pavilion
6	Connecting arbor	13	Artist studio
7	Shade ramada	14	Hobby center

Purpose, Permanence and Value: *The built environment not only radiates what was valued at the time it was built but how it will be valued in the future. The whole concept of community requires a commitment to place that transcends any one use or lifetime. Personal interests and circumstances will continue to change, but what we build should have a more lasting relationship to its context. These three images each convey a sense of their purpose, permanence and value. Lovingly created structures and places fare far better over time than anything expedient. The expedient is at its best when new. The authentic, being neither new nor old, becomes richer with the patina of age. Its timelessness is more like that of nature itself—a beauty that exists outside the stylistic preferences of any one time or place. To create the authentic is to create the heritage we leave for the future, just as those we admire from the past have done for us.*

150

Use of Color: *Some wonderful places are very muted, others are multicolored or multitoned. While there is no one right color scheme, there should always be a guiding idea. Like a fine painting, what we ultimately experience and value most is not any one element but the effect of the overall composition.*

153

Urban Limit Lines

One of the more tangible devices of the new effort toward "smart growth" is the establishment of urban limit lines. If we are to establish physical boundaries to growth, instead of being merely bureaucratic lines to control the phasing of available land, let them be formative edges as inviolate as the shorelines of the Great Lakes. Whether following natural features or designed patterns, these open spaces should not only be "preserves" for their own sake, but also a connective tissue for the community. New York's Central Park, the canals of Venice and the most satisfying urban designs around the world provide convincing examples of permanent open spaces that combine character and beauty with human utility.

Regional Open Space

Regional open-space networks should be designed with as much or more intention as would be accorded to the urban design of a city or the comprehensive routing of a regional transportation system. Unlike urban limit lines, which are most often used to discipline the timing of development, regional open space should be permanent. And unlike special-purpose "preserves," which often occur at the community's edge, the most effective open-space systems will provide an internal armature around which all other land use and circulation patterns are designed to occur. Tomorrow's regional networks will combine natural features, including sensitive topography, valuable vegetation, wildlife habitats and wetlands with connecting corridors that weave in and around all present and future development. Conservation groups, private landowners, developers and municipalities are beginning to create alliances that address everything from agriculture and ranching to a more ecological approach to the design of golf courses, wetlands, gardens and natural systems for water reclamation. As this exploration continues, it will be in the best interests of all concerned to treat preservation, ownership and use as related but separate considerations. Open-space networks for the future will become the single most dominant characteristic of their respective communities. Regional open-space networks should be planned to be approximately equal in size to their corresponding urbanized areas.

Soverio deBu

The Venice Phenomenon

If places like Disney World, Epcot and even Celebration are theme parks reaching in the direction of idealized versions of real life, then Venice, an exceedingly real and historic community, is reaching in the direction of becoming a theme park. The resident population of Venice, which was once 270,000 people, is now down to 60,000 and decreasing, while 13,000,000 people annually visit what is arguably the earth's single most picturesque city.

The transition of Venice from community to tourist destination has many aspects that are no different from the well-known patterns of suburbia. The economy that once worked for its local citizenry can't compete with the invasion of tourist dollars. Little shops that once sold basic goods to locals have been replaced with multiple venues for everything from themed trinkets to high fashion retailers like Prada, Fendi, Versace and Armani. While there are no cars in Venice, they are nearby in an enormous, multi-level parking garage accessed by boat. This is the jumping-off point where Venetians, not unlike their suburban counterparts, become auto-dependant as they drive to the nearby city of Mestre to shop at a big-box supermarket.

Many of the living units in Venice are now being purchased by wealthy non-residents and thus remain unoccupied between visits. The result is that an ever-increasing number of Venetians are priced out of the market as local real estate is purchased by visitors and a variety of commercial interests. Not surprisingly, there is a tendency for those who consider themselves true Venetians to remain in separate societies from those who have simply come to live in Venice. While both its history and especially its beautiful architecture and waterways are undeniably unique, its human dynamics are all too familiar. High among the reasons cited by native Venetians who remain is the quality of life in which a stroll from work to home may take 10 minutes or two hours, depending upon how many friends they may meet along the way. But young people who want parks and ball fields, discos or other places to party, as well as individuals who harbor an entrepreneurial urge, leave Venice's historically significant setting for places that offer greater opportunity.

Perhaps the greatest lesson to learn from Venice is that even the most established, picturesque places on earth are subject to the same continually changing dynamics that no force can stop. Whatever we create for today will always be in the process of becoming. Rather than trying to arrest change, the best designs and the most vibrant communities accept change as natural and plan accordingly. The nostalgic and the picturesque will always have their appeal, but they will never replace the certain need to address how we really live.

"To think that people could revert to traditional, pre-industrial villages was a fantasy, even as it was impossible to ignore some people's hopes of having more traditional towns... Places like Seaside or Celebration are not 'real' in the sense of being fully operating villages, autonomous economically and culturally in the 19th-century sense. Plainly, they are not. They depend on tourists and rentals, and on highways to carry the inhabitants away to jobs and hospitals and grocery stores."

– Charles W. Moore
You Have to Pay for the Public Life

Florentine and Venetian Infill: *The wealthy families of the 12th and 13th centuries built their free-standing, towering homes, each wanting theirs to be the highest. Additional houses were eventually built in between the first structures, creating a fabric of related façades. Lines where the individual structures now intersect remain clearly visible.*

"Venice is becoming a beautiful museum and a fine place for the carnival, but it is no longer a real, living city."

– Gherardo Ortalli
Professor of Medieval History
University of Venice

Public Art

People don't generally describe what they do by saying, "I'm a genius," but throngs of people say, "I'm an artist." Words that imply qualitative judgments like "genius" and "artist" would seem better left to be conferred by others, using instead more accurate descriptors like, "I am a painter, dancer, actor, sculptor, writer or musician."

The term "artist" can be particularly troublesome when "public art" is mandated by law and funded with dollars that would otherwise go to whatever is being built. In the worst of cases it has produced what critics have judged to be rarely public, rarely art. Also problematic is the assumption that neither the architecture nor its setting can be considered art, for if they were, there would be no need to allocate one percent of the budget for a special achievement that a selection committee has proclaimed to be "art." Again, if to be "art" means it must be something other than the design of the totality, why not state clearly that one percent of the budget will be allocated for paintings, sculpture, murals or some form of staged or interactive performance? That would at least remove the pretense.

In keeping with current widespread practices, public art is allowed to be just about anything but that created by either the architect or landscape architect. This issue is raised to encourage the thought that our greatest works of art might one day again be our cities. There is no reason why we shouldn't aspire to create in the future what novelist Evelyn Waugh once said of Venice: "It is in itself the greatest surviving work of art in the world."

Unlike that featured in a museum, where the purpose is to expose, educate, explore, stretch and possibly even shock our sensibilities during occasional visits of our own choosing, and unlike the totally personal prerogatives of the private collector, public art, by its very purpose, has a context of community immersion not of its own making. It is not something on display within an environment designed for study, it is the environment. Thus to qualify as public art, considerations for the spatial relationships of context should be as significant as the artifact itself.

Ghiberti's Doors of Paradise, Florence

"By artist I mean of course everyone who has tried to create something which was not here before him, with no other tools and material than the uncommercial ones of the human spirit."

– William Faulkner

Examples abound where so-called public art is far more an expression of someone's idiosyncratic notions than anything to do with its spatial purpose or place. Often the result of such installations achieves nothing more than a brief moment of controversy followed by quick descent into obscurity.

In addition to context, another guideline for public art would be that it should inspire public engagement beyond whatever merit it may have as an artifact on its own. The goal is for public art to be conceived with respect for the scale, pace and frequency with which it is viewed. It must inspire engagement at a more integrated level of community than that of an exhibit-like presentation.

This two-part criterion can be satisfied by anything from animating a space to something more independent but powerful enough for its presence to be felt by the community. Like the magic one feels from the changing patterns of sunlight, public art may also be more ephemeral, including events in which citizen involvement becomes inseparable from the work itself.

Regenerating the Primitive

WaterFire Providence is public art at its most viscerally powerful and effective. A multimedia installation created by artist Barnaby Evans, WaterFire was originally designed as part of the Rhode Island capital city's 1995 First Night festivities. Since then, it has become a nationally recognized ongoing event with dozens of "lightings" during spring, summer and fall.

WaterFire became a symbol of Providence's renaissance. It was instrumental in enlivening a once deteriorating downtown and transforming Providence's image from aging industrial city to dynamic cultural center. Each season, nearly a million visitors and residents flock to the banks of Providence's rivers to take part in this celebration of beauty and rebirth.

Much of the magic of WaterFire is evident in its name. The alchemy of the elemental, of bright, raging flames upon flowing water, is something that speaks to every soul on the most fundamental level. Heart-stirring music from all over the world is heard along the banks during the lightings, sweeping participants and observers into a kind of magical moment in time, light-years removed from the ordinary demands of daily life. Downtown shops, restaurants and sidewalk vendors stay open late, and people can eat, drink, smell, touch and buy to their heart's content. WaterFire evenings present a true feast for the senses, a time and place for celebration and community without reservations.

This powerful combination of ritual, art and community is not limited by time or place. Like fire itself, it is the magic of light and warmth, all designed to be passed along and shared. WaterFire exemplifies the meaning of public art. It is a beauty that speaks to us as individuals while also drawing us closer together in recognition of the shared wonder of the imaginative and timeless beauty that exists for us to share.

The Art of Engagement: *Fires burn before the civic facilities of Memorial Park, the Providence County Superior Courthouse and the famous Rhode Island School of Design. The result is a grand proximity, both physically and spiritually, between art and politics, beauty and business.*

Everybody's Treasure: *Gondolas ferry visitors through the flames, while WaterFire's five boats, each named after characters from Greek mythology, silently tend the flames. Community volunteers pilot and crew the wood boats that glide along the rivers from sunset until past midnight, lighting and stoking the bonfires. Each year, hundreds of Providence residents add their names to a waiting list, eager to contribute to something that has given their city so much. In whatever form it takes, a significant measure of public art should be that it achieves a sense of communal ownership—becoming a treasure worthy of the community's care, time, energy and protection.*

Milwaukee Art Museum

American Folk Art Museum

The Art of Architecture: *We would not call all buildings great works of art any more than we would automatically confer that distinction to all music, dance, paintings or sculpture. But when the forms, spaces, systems and materials are so artfully conceived as to transcend mere function, should they not be considered to be among our greatest works of public art? Such structures become large-scale compositions of space that can be experienced from within and without, changing by day and by night, unfolding their mysteries even more with the seasons and, ultimately, reflecting the patina of generations.*

Earth, Light and Space: *This desert complex literally grew out of the earth of which it is now an inseparable feature. Soil from its site was compressed into massive forms. Shade is provided by tensile sails as old as the tents of desert nomads and as new as their 21st-century materials. These earthen forms and tent-like canopies, together with the use of native vegetation and the cooling effect of water, are all about connections—between materials of the past and technologies of the future, between interior and exterior space, and between the surprise of spaces, vistas and areas that encourage interaction. Settings of beauty are essential to an enduring sense of community.*

Heroic
Commitment

SIX

*"Instinctively and naturally if you
beautify your own life, you beautify
the life of everyone around you.
We share it, we get from it, it belongs to us."*

– Frank Lloyd Wright

Designing With Nature

In deference to nature, we have created a variety of ordinances that limit human behavior. We have ordinances that protect wildlife, vegetation, wetlands and hillsides, as well as those that protect each of us from the rest of us. This network of limitations once prompted Buckminster Fuller to say that the advances upon which all of society depends are developed in what he called "the outlaw area." His definition of the outlaw area was any place—for example, at sea beyond the three-mile limit—where our building codes, laws and other imposed limits had not yet replaced invention and the creative process with rules and standards.

To those who write or administer generic ordinances, the idea of respecting the natural environment generally means some version of "don't touch it." This is understandable, for how could it be any other way? What more sensitive treatment could their imaginations entertain? Since one of the primary purposes of such ordinances is to prevent abuse, it is inevitable that they also limit anything sufficiently special to need consideration on its own merits.

The challenge of the 21st century is not only to preserve natural habitat but to create structures and settlements that celebrate their surroundings in ways that lift the human spirit. Beautiful places exert an emotional pull on the soul. We are beginning to understand that the creative contribution of humanity is a critical component of nature itself.

In a beautiful community, most of the structures should be experienced as background, just as most trees in a landscape or brush strokes in a painting or notes in a symphony do not call undue attention to themselves. So it must be with the structures of a well-considered community. But background is only part of the story. Think of the places that continue to inspire the imagination with their timeless beauty. King Ludwig II's Neuschwanstein Castle and the hillside villages of Italy and France all occupy sensitive settings, but it is their own beauty that we admire most. In the Americas, the ruins of Mesa Verde and the historic sanctuary of Machu Picchu provide enduring records of human mastery.

The Special Case

Structures that reflect extraordinary commitment are among the highest expressions of human achievement. Without them there can be no culture. Thus, they are a necessary part of an empowered community.

Fallingwater in Bear Run, Pennsylvania, shown on the facing page, is one of the most famous houses in the world. In David Pearson's book, *Earth to Spirit: In Search of Natural Architecture*, he writes, "Frank Lloyd Wright always attempted to build in harmony with the land. Completed in 1936, Fallingwater is the archetypal expression of Wright's spirit of the land and sense of place. Perched over the Bear Run waterfall, the building's various cantilevered levels glide over the water like the branches of a tree." Such sentiments frequently accorded to Fallingwater are certainly deserved, but they also raise an important question about how our approval process would treat such an extraordinary design if it were proposed today.

The design of Fallingwater consists of huge slabs of reinforced concrete cantilevered over a waterfall. Large concrete footings are anchored directly into the stream bed itself. If the house did not already exist, how many of today's environmentalists would lend their enthusiastic endorsement? I would guess the answer would be very few, if any. A more likely response would be, "Mr. Wright, I'm sure this would be a beautiful structure, but if we let you get away with it we would have to let the next guy do it too. And the next guy may not be as sensitive as you are." This is the familiar catch-22. Since we can't make everyone equally great, we choose to make everything equally mediocre. The price we pay for this leveling is extraordinary, yet no one is held accountable for the loss. However we do it, the safety nets we devise for our protection must not be allowed to become barriers that preclude our most expansive creative potential.

We inhabit the earth against a background of great human endeavor. We stand on the shoulders of everything from the ancient settlements of the Anasazi to all that subsequent generations have created at their best. We are at a pivotal moment in history and are fully capable of designing with unprecedented sensitivity and effectiveness. We have an enlightened citizenry, and the capability of our builders and developers is second to none. Our democratic institutions have had more than 200 years of trial and error, and the creativity of our design professionals has never been more ready for greatness. All that remains is to raise our level of dialogue to where we both expect and permit the extraordinary.

The 21st century will either find less use for the term environmentalist or become more demanding as to what it is meant to describe. At the end of the 20th century, we had pretty much rendered it meaningless by applying it to those whose dedication is to understand the puzzling complexities of nature's integrated systems, as well as to those having absolutely no credentials other than whatever personal prejudices they may have held at any given moment. The first represents a treasure of scientific inquiry at its most needed, the latter is nothing but wasteful obstruction.

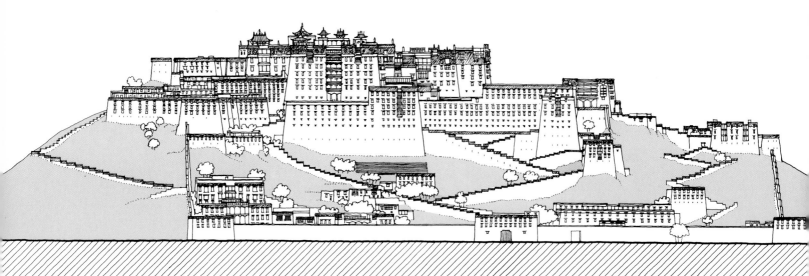

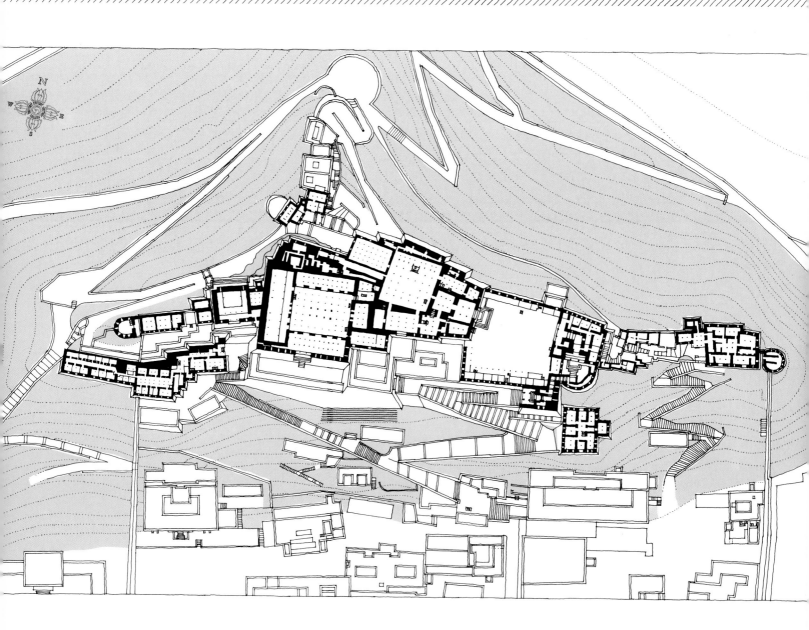

The Potala in Lhasa, Tibet: *Both precise line drawings of The Potala and photos of its three-dimensional structure display an unmistakable grandeur that not only respects but adds to the mystery and majesty of the land. If we are willing to believe that what we build goes beyond our own usage to convey a message to others, what the greatest works convey will always be a testimony to the enduring power and creativity of the human spirit. To build with greatness should not be confused with exaggeration or grandiosity. From the beginning of time, humanity's most treasured creations have always added to the beauty of their sensitive settings. In any area of achievement, at the very highest level, the examples are few. What the special solution represents can never be all things to all people. But while humanity's finest may never exemplify our need for "standards," the value of the special case is to provide inspiration for raising the level of the rest.*

Machu Picchu: *The ancient city of Machu Picchu is one of the great mountain communities of all time. More than 200 structures were terraced into a cascade of connecting levels, including two towns, one at a higher elevation than the other. The city was built in the 15th century and rediscovered in 1911. Known as the Lost City of the Incas, it stands as an inspiring example of the transformation of human ingenuity into a work of natural beauty.*

Mesa Verde: *The ancients combined boldness with sensitivity. More than 2,000 years ago, the Anasazi designed structures in harmony with their natural settings, leaving those settings more beautiful than they found them. The lessons left behind at Cliff Palace are many. The Anasazi built intelligently with respect to the elements, and what they built provided for the complexity and integration of community.*

Greatness Requires Context

In addition to providing for our collective needs, community is the vehicle for increasing our effectiveness. What humanity associates with personal greatness is as dependent on community as it is on the individual. To think otherwise would be to have Shakespeare without a stage, Frank Lloyd Wright without the opportunity to build, Andrew Lloyd Webber without an orchestra and Michael Jordan without a team.

I have played the trumpet since I was 7 years old. In my early twenties I had the life-enriching opportunity to study with Adolph Herseth, who symphonic musicians refer to as "Bud." Herseth is a legend among brass players, and many regard him to be the greatest symphonic trumpet player of all time. *The New York Times* once referred to him as "quite possibly the most dazzling player in the world today." Herseth was given the coveted role of principal trumpet with the Chicago Symphony when he was just 27 years old, a position he held until he retired 53 years later, just short of his 80th birthday.

During one of my lessons, Herseth explained that he would never practice a solo in his own studio, because he didn't want to allow the feeling and sound to get set in his mind at a level he could produce alone. Instead, he wanted to remain open to the inspiration of the orchestra. In seeing himself as part of the greater totality, he would respond at a level of performance beyond anything he might otherwise achieve. This explanation has stuck with me as a powerful symbol of mutual advantage—Bud Herseth, as individual, the Chicago Symphony as community, each contributing to the greatness of the other.

Artful Achievements

Whether for purposes of making great music or great communities, heroic performance is all about nurturing the highest expressions of human achievement. Without them, there can be no culture. The most special places are those that demonstrate their appropriateness to the land, to the time and to the people. They call upon our ability to distinguish between the truly beautiful and that which is merely expedient.

New York's Central Park, designed by Frederick Law Olmsted and Calvert Vaux, provides an extraordinary example of heroic design. Built in two phases between 1858 and 1873, the 843-acre park is a thoroughly constructed landscape. It exemplifies Frank Lloyd Wright's thesis that, "What is natural may not be architectural, but what is architectural must always be natural." Transformed by the artistry and technology born of human imagination, Central Park exists as a celebration of natural beauty beyond anything the land represented in its untouched state. It is one thing to protect the environment by proclaiming our most sensitive sites off limits. It is a far higher calling to rise to the challenge by creating artful environments. It is all a matter of rising above the norm and having the insights and courage to create the exceptional.

Central Park

Consider what it took for this spectacular human achievement to exist. Land had to be assembled, wetlands filled, hills created and lakes dug. Endeavoring to do that today would require breaking through all manner of constraints, which is exactly what we must do whenever justified by the opportunity. The excerpt on the facing page is taken from an open letter that appeared in *Garden Design* magazine. It was written by Dorothy Kalins, the magazine's editor in chief. Her expression of gratitude for the human values of Central Park describe the sustaining gift of design that can only occur when heroic insights are supported by long-term commitments.

The following paragraphs are from the proposed plan that was awarded first prize by the Board of Commissioners of the Central Park on April 28, 1858.

"The park throughout is a single work of art and, as such, subject to the primary law of every work of art, namely, that it shall be framed upon a single, noble motive, to which the design of all its parts, in some more or less subtle way, shall be confluent and helpful.

"It is one great purpose of the park to supply to the hundreds of thousands of tired workers, who have no opportunity to spend their summers in the country, a specimen of God's handiwork that shall be to them, inexpensively, what a month or two in the White Mountains or the Adirondacks is, at great cost, to those in easier circumstances."

"Dear Mr. Olmsted:

"How did you know the power of that landscape to connect a city to its humanity? ...How could you see meadows and wide pools and waves of trees and low shrubs for bird cover and endless, rolling greens?

"Where did you find the chutzpah and the courage to sculpt ... sensuous hillsides, to plant heroic trees, to dig deep ponds, to scrape earth away from huge rocks, or move them—all as easily as shaping sand on the beach? And how did you make it look as though it had always been there?

"How could you know that sinking the transverse roads so pedestrians would be safe and milk wagons could pass, virtually undetected, would still work today for fuming buses and howling Harleys? How could you ... have understood the sociology of play areas that would attract countless generations of families and children of every sort? How could you ... have foreseen the healing power that the first hopeful drifts of daffodils have on a winter-dark city?

"How could you, so long ago, have given us a place so ever-changing that it never twice looks the same no matter how many times I pass by or how many scenes of life I've played out there? I will never understand it. But I am so grateful you did."

Villa d'Este

Begun in the 16th century, the fountains and gardens of Villa d'Este stand as tribute to the sustaining power of beauty. The estate was developed and nurtured through tumultuous times, passing from one generation to the next and from one family to another before becoming property of the Italian state. The gardens had to live through World War I and were actually bombed during World War II. Horrendous conflicts have come and gone while the beauty lives on. Not many of us will have the opportunity to build our own Villa d'Este, but we can all appreciate its artistry and ongoing stewardship. Wherever the fortunes and discernment of a few have come together on the land, something is added to the world that enriches life for all of us.

Working With the Terrain: *The image on the facing page is from a medieval town in Italy and shown above is a contemporary commercial district in Mexico. In both examples, the natural topography is used not only to address utilitarian purposes but to achieve something memorably beautiful. It is in this "best of both worlds" that form and function become one.*

Variance for Excellence

If we are serious about getting beyond the dreariness of ordinance and production-driven sameness, we must be willing to consider more creative patterns of development. Imagine the above setting without any structures. Now imagine that a rezoning sign appears and you learn that a developer intends to grade the hill into a series of terraces for walks, streets and a wide variety of houses, all as shown in the photograph. With our code-enforced prohibitions against anything that isn't routine, how many of the dramatic places we travel thousands of miles to admire would we allow to be built today? To leave sensitive settings untouched is certainly better than to develop them poorly. But to build with creative boldness is to add to the beauty of the land. Must our codes and ordinances not only preclude the worst but also the best? Why not a variance for excellence, so human imagination might join forces with nature, as has so often happened in the past? Artful design radiates a look that tells a story. There is a visual sense of agreement in form, color, materials and landscaping. It is an authentic character that can be felt in everything from a distant view to the more intimate sense of streets and gardens. Given our financial strength and superior tools, we must surely regret how seldom we make such beauty a part of our everyday experience.

The Role of Religion

The subject of religion is not only pervasive but so personal that it might be regarded as an unwise distraction in a book about community. That would be easier to conclude if the whole of human history, despite its documented periods of brutality, didn't point to religion as a consistent element of the social order.

Huston Smith is a remarkable man who spent more than a half century exploring the world's great religions, not as competing theologies, but to get to what he calls the "water table" of their similarly significant missions. Having immersed himself for approximately 10 years each in the study of Hinduism, Buddhism, Confucianism, Christianity, Judaism and Islam, he offers two conclusions, both of which are inseparable from the history of community.

The first is that all the great religions, at their core, are cultivators of the uniquely human virtues of "intelligence, compassion, creativity, beauty and goodness." The second is that those who devote their lives to such studies have yet to find any record of a civilization that didn't have a religious component so thoroughly woven into the social fabric of the time that it is impossible to isolate it as an independent element.

I relate strongly to Smith's observations. My own sense of exploration and mission was shaped from the cradle by the religious integrity of a mother and father who practiced what they preached. I regard this early influence to be both a precious gift as well as an intellectual and emotional ferment so intense that it remains more of a lifelong mystery to be lived than anything capable of being solved.

The Search for Truth

In a 1957 television interview, Mike Wallace asked Frank Lloyd Wright what he thought of organized religion. Wright's response was, "Why organize it?" That would be my question as well, except that all ideas for living, however they start, either die out or become institutionalized. There is no question that organizational strength can contribute greatly to longevity. Its weakness is the tendency to favor managed ritual over the continued search for truth.

The 1931 Nobel Peace Prize Laureate Nicholas Murray Butler used to insist that at some moment in the Garden of Eden, Adam turned to Eve and said, "I can't escape the feeling that we're living in a time of transition." This is a feeling we would all do well to make a centerpiece of life.

Wherever two or more people come in contact, it is necessary to establish a balance between private desires and shared responsibilities—individuality and community. This balance is an ever-changing flow—something for which we are all players in the present without knowing what we are part of becoming in the future.

The Glue of Society

History continues to show that how we treat our religious beliefs can either bring us into community or drive us apart. I've always liked the words of Justice Oliver Wendell Holmes, who said that his religion consisted of "the first two words of the Lord's Prayer," or Ralph Waldo Emerson, who said, "Let a man keep the law, *any law*, and his life will go better for it."

A doctrine-free definition of religion might be that it is a force that can be felt by humans at a far deeper level than any other influence. This unparalleled power is impossible to understand but easy to describe. It is a connection between what we can know at any given time and everything beyond that. The wealthiest, most intelligent and meticulously organized people on earth know that all such certainties are left behind with their last breath, and none of us know when that will occur.

The world only "works" because most people are "good" and that which is good about humanity relates to beliefs and allegiances that go beyond the rule of law. No law is needed to inspire compassion, nor would it be possible to conceive of one that could.

While it is likely that most people think of religion in far different terms from those associated with business and government, it nonetheless has a pervasive influence over the values of society. In his book *Excellence: Can We Be Equal and Excellent Too?*, John W. Gardner extols the virtue of the individual pursuit of excellence under democracy, as opposed to living under a social order where birth determines occupation and status.

Gardner observes that, "One doesn't give the Prince of Wales an aptitude test and start him in the stock room," and goes on to say that it took more than the power of the Industrial Revolution to bring "a new measure of autonomy to the individual." He credits the emergence in the United States of "religious ideas that laid great stress on individual responsibility."

This book is not the place to advance the discussion of religion for its own sake, however to omit its deeper influence from our thoughts about community would be to ignore what many see as the glue of societal order. If humanity couldn't count on people who are willing to take great risks, we would still be crowding in caves. If there were no instinctive and even mysterious feelings about something more and better than what already exists, there would be no reason to take risks. And if it weren't for the fact that most people are "good," there wouldn't be enough police, walls, locks, jails and armies in the world to keep the peace. The common denominator of religion is that it provides a connection between decent, caring behavior in the here and now with the unknowable realities of our births and deaths, and so much that is puzzling in between.

While each generation makes its own decisions as to what to do with the wisdom of the ages, there is hardly an enduring institution worth mentioning—including our finest hospitals, colleges and universities, as well as the United States of America itself—that doesn't owe its existence to the pursuit of values that are more rooted in a religious sense of purpose than any more pragmatic explanation.

"All the strength and force of a man comes from his faith in things unseen. He who believes is strong; he who doubts is weak. Strong convictions precede great actions."

– James Freeman Clarke

"...It is a strange thing that most of the feeling we call religious, most of the mystical outcrying which is one of the most prized and used and desired reactions for our species, is really the understanding and the attempt to say that man is related to the whole thing, related inextricably to all reality, known and unknowable. This is a simple thing to say, but a profound feeling of it made a Jesus, a St. Augustine, a Roger Bacon, a Charles Darwin, an Einstein. Each of them in his own tempo and with his own voice discovered and reaffirmed with astonishment the knowledge that all things are one thing and that one thing is all things..."

– John Steinbeck

"He to whom the emotion is a stranger, who can no longer pause to wonder and stand wrapped in awe, is as good as dead; his eyes are closed. To know what really exists, manifesting itself as the highest wisdom and the most radiant beauty, which all our dull faculties can comprehend only in their most primitive form—this knowledge, this feeling is at the center of true religiousness."

– Albert Einstein

"If we take the world's enduring religions at their best, we discover the distilled wisdom of the human race."

– Huston Smith

"Wisdom clearly is to believe what one desires; for belief is one of the indispensable preliminary conditions of the realization of its object. Faith creates its own verification. Believe, and you shall be right, for you shall save yourself; doubt, and you shall again be right, for you shall perish. The only difference is that to believe is greatly to your advantage."

– William James

"The man with an idea has been a Mohammed, a Jesus, a Lao-tze, a Buddha..."

– Frank Lloyd Wright

"In the end, like the Almighty Himself, we make everything in our own image for want of a more reliable model; our artifacts tell more about ourselves than our confessions."

– Joseph Brodsky

"Conscience is the guardian in the individual of the rules which community has evolved for its own preservation."

– William Somerset Maugham

Multi-Generational Commitment

The building of a single structure, the Santa Maria del Fiore cathedral in Florence, provided the livelihood for an entire community during the 140 years it took to complete. Its celebrated dome, designed by Filippo Brunelleschi, is made up of 37,000 tons of stone. The cathedral had been under construction for more than a century before the dome was even started. Most remarkable of all, the dome was under construction for decades before anyone was able to demonstrate a structural concept that would permit its completion. The power of belief behind this masterpiece was so strong that the details were assumed to be solved as the work progressed. Last but not least, the building of this miracle of human genius was built by generations of ordinary citizens, despite a background of war and intrigue. More than five-and-a-half centuries after its completion, the cathedral and its Florentine setting continue to inspire those who visit, photograph and make paintings of its sculptural beauty. Both the cathedral and Florence itself are under continual restoration—a testament to the eternal quality of greatness.

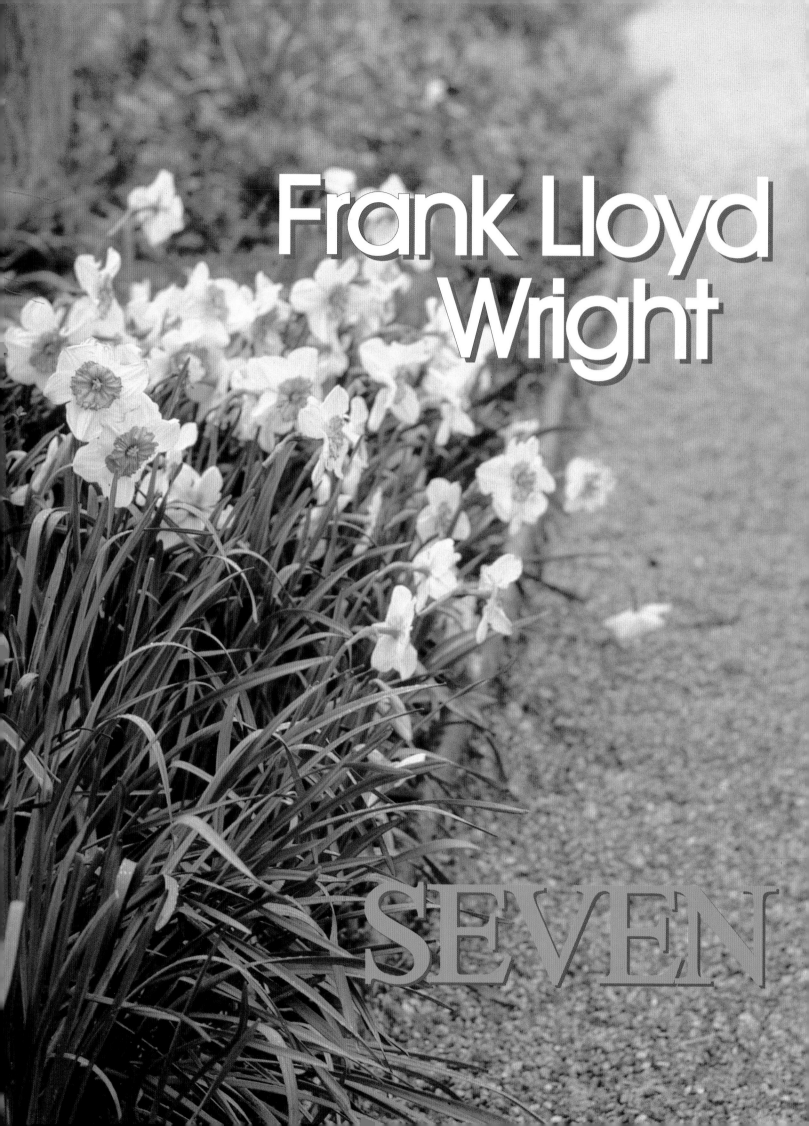

Frank Lloyd Wright

SEVEN

*"True human culture has a healthy sense of the beautiful...
nobly relating man to his environment. The sense of this
natural aesthetic would make of man a gracious, integral,
potent part of the whole of human life."*

– Frank Lloyd Wright

An American Original

A half century after his death, Frank Lloyd Wright's architecture coupled with the deeply human philosophy of his writings continue to inspire new books, seminars, plays and even an opera. He believed culture to be at its best when authentic to its own time and place. Wright dedicated himself to expressing the heroic, youthful spirit of American democracy.

While others imitated anything they could copy from the Greeks, Romans and English, Wright stayed true to his thesis, applying it to everything from houses, structures and furnishings, to the way we organize our relationships with each other, including the elements of community and nature itself.

The integrity of his seven decades of exploration is all the more remarkable when compared to the far easier practice of settling for nostalgia and imitation. At the other extreme, Wright never succumbed to the equally easy pursuit of designs that are more novel than significant. Even at their most dramatic, his "effects" were the result of thoughtful purpose. A good example is New York's Guggenheim Museum, where every line and surface of the sculptural exterior is an honest consequence of its interior purpose, space and flow.

Another good example of architectural integrity between interior purpose and exterior form can be seen below in Wright's light-filled design for the Beth Sholom Synagogue in Elkins Park, Pennsylvania.

Culture and Community

I have often been asked to describe my sense of Frank Lloyd Wright's most lasting affect on his apprentices. While there is no one answer, there are two broad categories. The first is the influence on those for whom the look of Wright's architecture is reflected in their own. The other influence is less obvious. Rather than being focused on his highly personal designs, the second category is made up of those for whom Wright's ideas and ideals are the more dominant influence. An example of his philosophy can be felt in the sentiment to the right, which reflects the kind of thinking he shared with his apprentices. For anyone who was there to hear him, the feeling was one of being both challenged and inspired. What he spoke represented the life commitment of a man who had lived his every word and, in the process, somehow managed to interest much of the world in what he had to say.

"Consider that you, as young architects, are to be the pattern-givers of civilization. If we ever do have a culture of our own, you must provide the vision. A civilization is only a way of life. A culture is the way of making that way of life beautiful. So culture is your office here in America, and as no stream can rise higher than its source, so you can rise no more or better to architecture than you are. So why not go to work on yourselves, to make yourselves, in quality, what you would have your buildings be?"

The author (seated) as a teenage apprentice with Frank Lloyd Wright in the Taliesin Drafting Room.

Broadacre City

Wright never stopped thinking about what form a city might take if inspired by our youthful democratic ideals. A hypothetical composite of his thoughts was first modeled in 1934. Six decades later, the model was reworked for a 1994 exhibit at New York's Museum of Modern Art. In all, he wrote four books dealing with his concept for a new way to design communities in harmony with the land, including *The Disappearing City*, *When Democracy Builds*, *The Living City* and *The Industrial Revolution Runs Away*.

Nearly half a century after Wright's death, it is common for bookstores that may have a volume or two on the most famous architects of the day to have an entire shelf dedicated to books about Frank Lloyd Wright. In spite of having received more attention, honors and accolades than any other architect, Wright has nonetheless been misunderstood by friend and foe alike. Nowhere is this more true than in his concepts for community which he called Broadacre City. Most contemporary scholars have either found little merit in Wright's planning or dismissed it as something too dominated by the rigors of architecture to qualify in the messier arena of what constitutes a city.

Wright's critics dismiss Broadacre City as being too simplistic to be worthy of consideration, and his followers inflict unintended harm by focusing on its details rather than seeing it for the deeper exploration of relationships between democracy, nature and habitation that Wright intended. The unhelpful believers are those who offer a literal interpretation for every model and sketch. This does nothing but prompt others to criticize what they see as lacking in cultural or ecological diversity or pointing out that the model shows inadequate parking, which leads them to judge that Wright greatly underestimated today's traffic volumes.

Quite clearly, Wright never intended for the entire nation to become a kind of ever-repeating patchwork quilt of his mainly flat, four-square-mile example. He was, after all, more than anyone before or since, someone whose work epitomized topographic and climate-responsive design. With respect to his understanding of increasing traffic volumes, he often said that every small town on earth could be destroyed by its own "success" if we didn't find ways to design more effective measures for transporting people, goods and services.

Wright offered five specific and related solutions of his own, including: 1) High-speed (200 mph) rail connections between population centers; 2) Artful arteries designed and engineered to accommodate the speeds that individual automobiles and trucks would one day travel; 3) The transmission of both liquid and dry goods in below-ground pipelines; 4) Full integration of all electronic communication for both voice and data, especially where possible to replace vehicular trips and, perhaps most important of all, 5) The need for the back-and-forth haul that we now call commuting. Wright wanted as many people as possible to live within walking distance of where they worked, something he and all who worked with him were able to do on a daily basis.

*Frank Lloyd Wright in 1935, working
on the model shown to the right*

Land Uses

1 County seat	25 Worship center
2 Airport	26 Guest houses
3 Stables and track	27 Research center
4 Sports fields	28 Arboretum
5 Baseball field	29 Zoo
6 Athletic clubs	30 Aquarium
7 Lake and stream	31 County fair
8 Small farms	32 Hotel
9 Custom residential	33 Country fair
10 Interior parks	34 Sanitarium
11 Music garden	35 Industrial units
12 Physical culture	36 Medical clinics
13 Market center	37 Apartments
14 Roadside inn	38 Dairy
15 Employee residential	39 Elementary school
16 Industry and dwellings	40 Taliesin equivalent
17 Commercial	41 Design center
18 Service businesses	42 Cinema
19 Main parkway	43 Forest cabins
20 Industry	44 Reservoir
21 Vineyards and orchards	45 Automobile objective
22 Live/work	46 Garages and stores
23 Residential	47 Gas stations
24 Schools	48 Educational center

A Growing Dynamic

"Broadacre City is certainly the most American scheme ever devised for our built environment, yet even today, 60 years after its inception, it remains an enigma to most laymen."

– H. Allen Brooks
Past President of the Society of
Architectural Historians

Many who discredit Broadacre City can only remember that Wright advocated an acre or more for every man, woman and child. What seemed then to be a revolutionary criterion has become today's norm. According to a Demographics Daily analysis of data from the 2000 Census, "all but 20 of America's 276 metropolitan areas have population densities of less than one person per acre." Another misconception is that Wright wanted everyone to live in a single-family dwelling. In fact, Wright's proposals were highly varied, including mid-rise buildings that combined office and living spaces on the same floor, clusters of fourplex units, and residential units over a variety of non-residential spaces.

In addition to it being the lifestyle choice of most Americans, decentralization is attracting support for new reasons. Renowned investor Warren Buffett, referring to the threat of terrorism within the United States, has suggested that, "This could slowly but surely lead to the de-urbanization of America." Buffet's observation has been echoed in newspaper articles by columnists and citizens alike, who have called for "a much higher spot on the national agenda for decentralization and energy independence. Each makes us less vulnerable to attack."

The words at the bottom of the preceding column were written by Dan Gillmor of the *San Jose Mercury News*. He goes on to make the case in a manner that is eerily similar to what Frank Lloyd Wright stated six decades ago:

"We need to spread out people and businesses by spreading out data and communications technology. Companies are putting backup data centers in distant places, a sensible approach, but this isn't enough. We need to give people and businesses a way to spread out in a more serious way, and we have the means if we're serious. Governments like choke points and ways to tap messages, but a decentralized system like the Internet is by definition more secure in the way that matters most—keeping communications running in times of crisis. It was no accident that on September 11, 2001, the most reliable message systems in New York were ones that used the packet-switching technology at the heart of the Internet.

"Decentralization is part of the energy-independence effort. Power generation today is mostly handled by massive plants, which are inevitable targets, and electricity moves on vulnerable lines. A move toward micro-power plants, solar energy and other such systems would not only be smarter, but safer."

Consider the following statement that Wright first published in 1932. "The skyscraper folly is no more. Our great cities have stopped growing. The regional field is duly increasing in size as transition to the countryside gets underway. The Aeroplane as a war engine makes it obvious that concentrations like cities are a menace to human life."

Going Forward

For the past seven decades, wherever the Broadacre models and drawings have been displayed, they have attracted and inspired large audiences. Wright's drawings and writings were always focused on ideas for living abundantly in special settings. In many ways, Broadacre City was the ultimate integration of what he most wanted to accomplish. The underlying philosophy revolved around living in harmony with nature and with each other. Wright saw architecture as being far more than physical design, and democracy as being far more than a form of government. Architecture and democracy were, for him, both about a way of life.

The next 10 pages portray Wright's exploration and commitment to his own expression of the Broadacre City ideal. It was manifested in the micro-communities he created at both Taliesin and Taliesin West. For 22 years, they served as my live/work laboratory, during which I never had need to own a car and probably consumed less energy in a year than the urban or suburban dweller uses in a month. The experience was healthful, educational and cultural.

Like all explorations in special-case settings, what I experienced at Taliesin and Taliesin West does not lend itself to outright replication. However, along with the other special places discussed in this book, each broadens our sense of what a community can be.

One of Broadacre City's land uses, shown as number 40 on page 194, is called The Taliesin Equivalent. Wright's dream was that others might explore and find their own ways to create thoughtful, artful places in which to live as fully and productively as he did until the day he died.

"Broadacre City is significant for the nature of its vision. It could probably not have occurred in just that way in any other country. It seized the American future, embodied it in a vision. The remarkable fact is just how visionary it proved to be."

– Peter Hall
Cities of Tomorrow

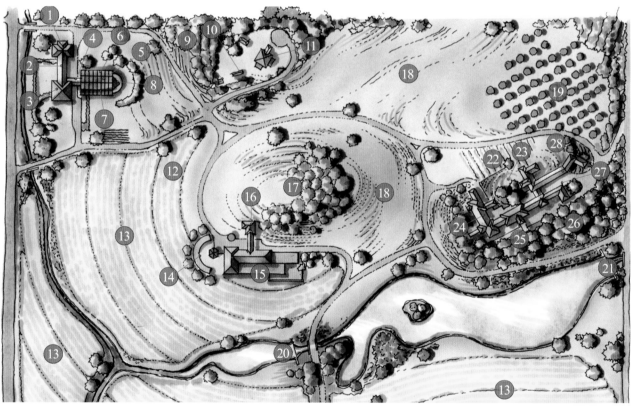

1 Hillside	8 "Tea" circle	15 "Midway" farm	22 Vineyard
2 Staff dining	9 Staff residences	16 Staff residence	23 Hill garden
3 Kitchen/living	10 "Romeo & Juliet"	17 Midway hill	24 Main residence
4 Bridge	11 Tan-Y-Deri	18 Pasture	25 Studio
5 Drafting room	12 Vegetable gardens	19 Orchard	26 Lower court
6 Staff quarters	13 Cultivated fields	20 Upper dam	27 Upper court
7 Staff quarters	14 Machinery shed	21 Lower dam	28 Staff residences

Taliesin: *The top photo shows three groupings of buildings, Hillside to the left, Midway in the center, and Taliesin itself on the right, facing out to man-made ponds which flow into the Wisconsin River. It is a panorama of commitment to the land, to the art of architecture and to the integration of community. The Midway farm buildings are shown above, and to the left is the lower dam.*

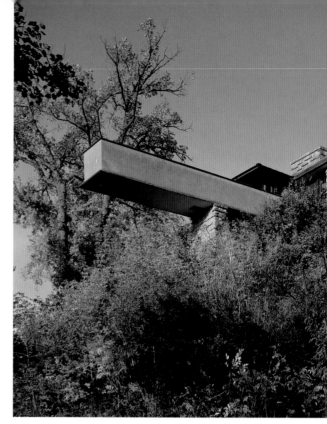

Fully Involved

Sculpture, pottery, architecture, construction, cooking and social activities were all part of the Taliesin day. The colored photo is a rehearsal for a dance drama for which the choreography and music were composed at Taliesin, as were the design and fabrication of the costumes and the graphic design of the programs, tickets and collateral materials. The Taliesin West Pavilion, designed by Wright, is shown under construction by his apprentices, who are also the dancers and musicians. And along the back wall is an exhibit of Wright's proposal for a new Arizona state capitol. While no single example will ever represent the perfect model for others, the central idea of the creative community is to provide tools, settings and opportunities that facilitate the ability to remain engaged in rewarding activities of one's own choosing.

Taliesin West

1 Parking
2 Shops
3 Offices
4 Entry forecourt
5 Main office
6 Theater cabaret
7 Music pavilion
8 Fountain
9 Pergola
10 Drafting room
11 Indian rock terrace
12 Pool
13 Private dining
14 Main kitchen
15 Staff dining
16 Guest deck
17 Staff apartments
18 Sunset terrace
19 Garden room
20 Main residence
21 Library
22 Staff quarters
23 Bridge
24 Guest house
25 Atrium
26 Staff quarters
27 Flower gardens
28 Citrus grove

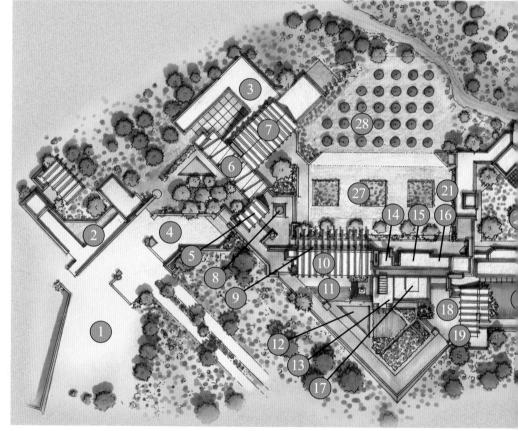

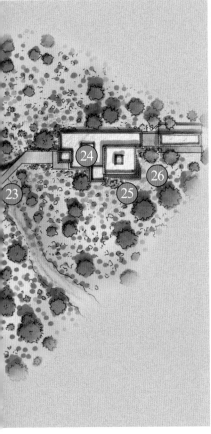

It Takes More Than Money

There are always those who discount anything beautiful or luxurious by saying, "All it takes is money," but that statement is false. For every accomplishment, there has been someone who nurtured a desire against the odds. Someone invested whatever time was necessary to refine and execute a desired outcome and, most of all, someone felt strongly enough to take the risk.

I was with Frank Lloyd Wright when a visiting scholar looked at one of his extraordinary designs and said, "All it takes is money." Wright was quick to respond, "You can't do much of anything without money, but money alone won't do it." The only enduring truth about money is that we all need it, and some people have more than others. However, the special contribution of design begins where such thoughts leave off. Design is the comprehensive search for insights that allow opportunities to be served in the best possible ways.

Nothing is more powerful for creating heritage than the imaginative use and stewardship of land. Building grandly is the American replacement for the inherited aristocracies of the past. Consider once again the examples of Taliesin and Taliesin West. In both locations, life was complete with museum-quality artwork, pottery, sculpture and Japanese screens. Pools, fountains and gardens were everywhere, including gardens for cutting flowers as well as gardens that provided fresh produce. Theaters were always alive with first-run movies, dramatic performances and live concerts.

In viewing the captioned photos of the communities Wright designed for himself and others, it may be inspiring to know that he was never in possession of great wealth. What's more, he didn't start building the Taliesin Fellowship in Wisconsin until he was 65, and in his seventies, he did it all over again in a totally different manner, creating the Taliesin West community in Arizona.

Education, Life and Work: *The buildings and grounds of Taliesin West combine in a single setting, with places for music, theater, work, study and residences for everyone involved. The architecture reaches beyond theories about style. Everything is designed to inspire commitment to culture, service and learning, all as lifelong ingredients of a rich existence.*

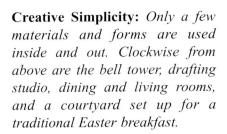

Creative Simplicity: *Only a few materials and forms are used inside and out. Clockwise from above are the bell tower, drafting studio, dining and living rooms, and a courtyard set up for a traditional Easter breakfast.*

DC Ranch

EIGHT

Designing for the Southwest

The 8,300-acre DC Ranch in Scottsdale, Arizona provides an example of conflict that was replaced by cooperation. The conflict began with a legal dispute between the owner of the property and the city that was settled by the Arizona Supreme Court in favor of the landowner. As part of the settlement, a master plan was established for the property. Legal battles are a less than ideal way to plan, and in this case, the master plan that came out of the court settlement would have led to a loss for both the natural environment and the future community. Fortunately, the property was given a second chance.

Five years after the court-generated plan was adopted, the entire planning process was repeated; only this time the developer and the city worked side by side to explore what it would take to create a quality community while still doing justice to the land. The result was a master plan that has been praised for its comprehensive architectural controls and governance, both of which extend well beyond practices of the past.

The process that produced the concept is worthy of discussion. From the start, the developer knew that the opportunity was exceptional and wanted the plan to reflect that reality. The planning effort was framed by three questions: 1) What was the logical next step for master-planned communities? 2) What were the people-centered amenities that would result in a diversity of neighborhoods? and 3) What would be the most effective mechanisms for design coherence, as well as ongoing guidance and governance? All elements of the community were linked by a system of paths and trails. The most sensitive hillside and mountain forms were protected in perpetuity. Related open space and controlled vistas were designed to weave throughout all developed areas.

Asking the right questions paved the way for a mix of residential types and densities to be within walking distance of a broad mix of urban services and community facilities. The plan combined the urban amenities of a town with the protected wildness of its mountain backdrop. It integrated the built environment with the natural setting, and enhanced each by the presence of the other. Everything started with an understanding of the land.

Celebrating the Desert: *For years, people have described the magnetism of the Southwest in terms of climate, but its attraction is far deeper, perhaps more in the realm of mystery. America's Sonoran desert is the richest, most diverse arid-region land in the world. Its atmospheric effects range from a somber sense of shelter to the surreal liquid fireworks of a flame-hued sunset. Its geology is youthful, angular and exposed. Its vegetation combines exotic skeletal geometry with the flowering of year-round color. From humanity's historic beginnings in the Mesopotamian Valley to the golf resorts of the Southwest, the atmosphere of the desert is spectacularly quiet. It is a place of vast views and feelings that seem to tap into a time when this land was inhabited by others. The challenge of creating community in the Sonoran desert is daunting, because nothing is ever covered up by tall trees and shrubs.*

210

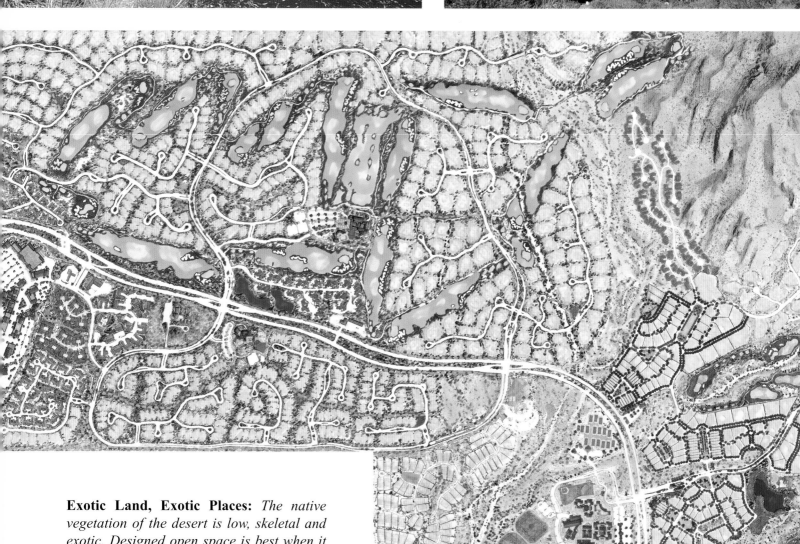

Exotic Land, Exotic Places: *The native vegetation of the desert is low, skeletal and exotic. Designed open space is best when it dramatizes the vastness of the land. Adding the open lands set aside for ownership by the city to open space designed as part of the development, as well as areas for recreation, a total of 6,128 acres, or 74 percent of the master plan consists of non-building areas. Of the remaining 26 percent, approximately half is in private gardens and other non-structural uses. The developed areas of DC Ranch are rich in flowering, drought-tolerant plantings and the use of moving water to create the cooling effect of an oasis.*

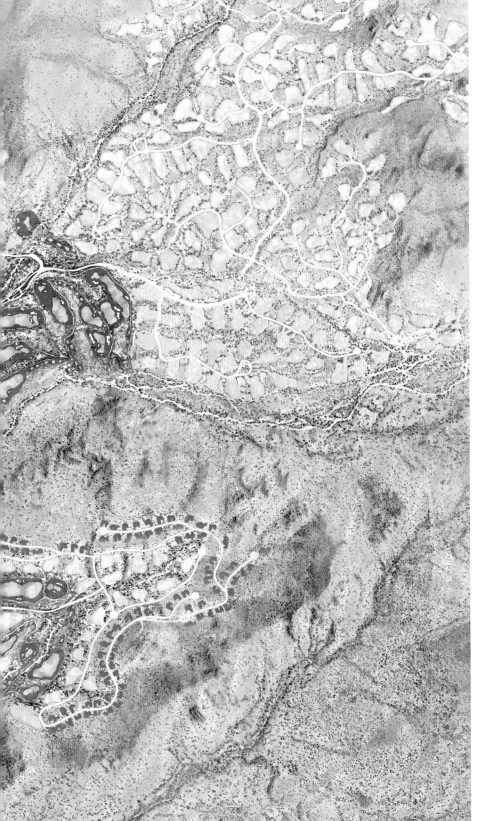

Refining the Vision

A sample yard was set up on-site to test a full range of colors and materials, including weathered steel, copper, integrally colored stucco, pavers, roof tiles, rammed earth and natural stone collected on the property.

Also tested were designs for a variety of walls, signage and lighting. The images on the facing page show everything from major monumentation and municipal signage to a bridge and bus stop, all of which are fitting expressions of their desert setting.

At the beginning of any master-planning assignment, relatively few people are focused on the totality. As the work proceeds, more and more people become engaged in smaller and smaller pieces of the overall concept. All but the most carefully nurtured ideas are at risk of being diminished as the process moves farther away from the clarity of the original vision.

The DC Ranch vision includes seven dissimilar but related commitments: 1) An overall framework of preserved natural features and open space; 2) A comprehensive mix of land uses related to vehicular and pedestrian circulation; 3) Topographic-sensitive site planning for each parcel; 4) An orchestrated design of all major structures; 5) Streets designed as architectural features, not just to satisfy engineering criteria; 6) A wide variety of housing types; and 7) The coordination of all urban design elements including, but not limited to, public spaces, bridges, lighting, signs, walls and fences.

Building in Character: *The architecture of DC Ranch observes a duality known to desert people since the beginning of time—the joy of living openly under the sky combined with the richness of and need for texture, shade, shadow and shelter from the sun. Simple walls, deep-set windows, overhangs, covered terraces and patios are all part of an authentic response to the desert environment. Exterior gardens become oasis settings, while the interiors are treated as a continuation of the colors, materials and character of the exterior.*

216

Staying On Message: *DC Ranch's visitors' center, school and community recreation areas each have their own character, but they are all component parts of the same symphony. They are all features of their Sonoran desert setting and, most importantly of all, to the citizens of the community, they are all "home." Just as one's house is more than any one room, in the true community, one's home extends far beyond any one house. While the luxury of living in community is ultimately a function of human interaction, it is greatly hindered or enriched by the design of all elements, both large and small. A good example of what it means to design in character with the land can be seen by comparing the architecture of DC Ranch with that of the Village of Kohler, Wisconsin that appears in the following chapter.*

218

Work, Shop and Play: *While the function and character of supermarkets, shops and offices differ widely from the purpose and elegance of a private country club, they are no less critical to the quality of the community. Commercial structures are far more likely to be compromised by the random elements of tenant needs, signage and the dictates of franchised operations. Such randomness is no more capable of contributing interest to the community than someone playing out of tune can add interest to the performance of a symphony. The images on this page are of the commercial district known as Market Street. On the facing page is one of the community's country clubs. While variety is evident in the differing functional requirements, the overall community has a cohesiveness that results from a consistent palette of materials, colors and character.*

220

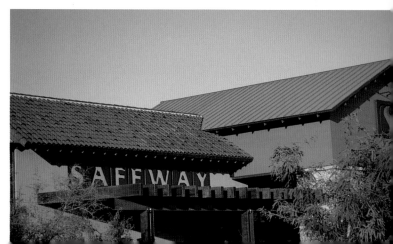

The Flow of Life: *The difference between planning for landscapes and structures as opposed to designing for life is the difference between developments that are merely picturesque and those that are focused on what happens after the development team has finished its work. Everything we plan, design and build should be conceived as a set of tools for enhancing human experience. The best planning and architecture becomes a living system that will be used, decorated and changed over time to support the needs and dreams of this and future generations. If when we design and develop we are willing to ask ourselves how this will all look and feel 10, 20 and more years from now, we will become more concerned with what matters and less limited by stylistic fashions of the day.*

223

The Village of Kohler

NINE

*"The Village of Kohler, Wisconsin
is an impressive example of first planning,
then following the plan... Every street
looks as if it had been designed
privately for its dwellers."*

– The New York Times, 1931

Creative Renewal

There are many places that owe their success to the developer's well-known mantras, "location, location, location," and "timing is everything." What distinguishes Kohler Village, in addition to its physical reality, is that it has little to do with the more typical market forces of location and timing, and everything to do with creating a context of excellence. It has never imitated the methods and formulas of others. In every respect, it is its own special place, beyond the reach of the conventional wisdom of market studies. And whenever such studies were performed, they often argued against what is now a living reality.

What the village represents more than anything is what we need more than anything—a renewed commitment to preserving heritage coupled with a dynamic commitment to the artful creation of community. For many reasons, not the least of which is the continuity of its stewardship, the Village of Kohler is a place where family pride, boldness and the democratic spirit are combined in a special ferment of never-ending exploration and design.

It is a place of deep respect for the past and a caring vision for the future. Its story is one of multi-generational commitment to the land, adaptive re-use of its historic structures and long-term creative investments that not only benefit the present but have been designed to sustain the community for generations to come.

An unmistakable characteristic of the Village of Kohler is its integration of the natural and built environments into an overall fabric of community. The American Club, a turn-of-the-century inn now on the National Register of Historic Places, has been lovingly restored to regenerate its original charm. The Village Center provides goods and services along with a lakeside inn. These features, complete with a 100,000-square-foot sports core and wooded area, surround a 12-acre lake within walking distance of a variety of residential neighborhoods. Seven miles of river wind through the heartland of the community, affording the setting for a 500-acre recreational and wildlife preserve.

The evolving quality of the village has been a seamless growth all adhering to its original plan, including periodic updates and eight decades of continuous architectural review. The village was incorporated from its inception and has since been governed by the many citizen officials who have served on its Planning Commission and Village Board, along with the multi-generational memory and continuity of its original developer, Kohler Co.

Expanding the Commitment

Among the most significant examples of planned communities are Frederick Law Olmsted's Riverside, Illinois (1869) and the English garden cities of Ebenezer Howard, including Letchworth (1903) and Welwyn (1919). Both Olmsted and Howard figured into the original planning for the Village of Kohler. The village was incorporated in 1913 and by 1916 the plan was described in a report as a "community that should be beautiful, good to live in, and American in spirit and government." Guiding this vision was Walter J. Kohler, then president of Kohler Co. He visited the Ebenezer Howard-inspired "garden cities" of Europe and America and retained the best planners and architects of his time.

In 1975, Herbert V. Kohler Jr., chairman, CEO and president of Kohler Co., set in motion a strategy for both preserving and expanding the original vision. He announced his plans, saying, "We have now reached the point in the growth of Kohler Village where it has become necessary to develop an overall plan to include practically all of the land now held by the corporation so that the continuity of an orderly development can be maintained."

The village had always been beautifully cared for by its residents, but had it not been regenerated by what is now called its "Second 50-Year Plan" it could have suffered the all too familiar decline of many Midwestern towns. My first visit to the village occurred during the summer of 1974. What I saw was a place of extraordinary commitment, great charm and obvious care. But significant structures had outlived their usefulness, and not unlike the experience of towns all over the country, the "mom-and-pop" shops had moved out to the nearby mall, the gas station moved out while I was standing there, and the American Club, a once proud building that housed immigrant workers until they could establish themselves, was underutilized and in a state of decay. The population was moving away, and those who stayed were getting older. There was a makeshift golf course with only five holes. Because of the community's high degree of maintenance, most of these issues remained largely invisible, but they were nonetheless real. That was more than 25 years ago. What has happened since is what one would wish for the regrettably many communities that fail to address the future with creative renewal.

The Kohler Village environment has all the charm and attributes of an American town at its most lovely, including distinguished buildings on the National Historic Register. The richness of the past has not only been restored and preserved but also regenerated into powerful expressions of community values for the future. A place where exemplary industry, education, shopping, recreation and resort hospitality coexist in a tapestry of public pathways, open space and tree-lined streets. As such, it accommodates the automobile but celebrates the human scale. It is a place where the diversity of individuality is balanced with the cohesiveness of architectural character. All are matters of design that require an allegiance to objectives far greater than simply making two-dimensional maps.

The Old and the New Are One: *Early village development was guided by a 50-year plan prepared by the Olmsted firm of Brookline, Massachusetts. The work of the firm's founder, Frederick Law Olmsted, is synonymous with this country's greatest places, stretching from Golden Gate Park in San Francisco to Central Park in New York. Subsequent development in the village has combined restoration and new construction into a seamless blend of the two.*

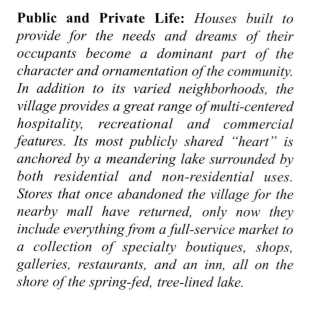

Public and Private Life: *Houses built to provide for the needs and dreams of their occupants become a dominant part of the character and ornamentation of the community. In addition to its varied neighborhoods, the village provides a great range of multi-centered hospitality, recreational and commercial features. Its most publicly shared "heart" is anchored by a meandering lake surrounded by both residential and non-residential uses. Stores that once abandoned the village for the nearby mall have returned, only now they include everything from a full-service market to a collection of specialty boutiques, shops, galleries, restaurants, and an inn, all on the shore of the spring-fed, tree-lined lake.*

228

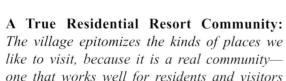

A True Residential Resort Community: *The village epitomizes the kinds of places we like to visit, because it is a real community— one that works well for residents and visitors alike. In addition to its neighborhoods and places of employment, it is a golf mecca, which includes two 18-hole courses known as Blackwolf Run (shown on the facing page) and another two 18-hole courses known as Whistling Straits. Golf Odyssey has called the combination of these courses "the best resort golf in the world."*

The Stewardship of Heritage: *The American Club, originally built in 1918 to house immigrant employees, is now a year-round destination resort and one of this country's most prestigious inns, having been honored as the Midwest's only AAA, Five Diamond resort hotel. The above middle photograph shows land being excavated for underground parking in order to create the expansive lawn shown immediately above. Another historic building, once the location for the community's stores, now houses the world-class Carriage House, Kohler Waters Spa, and the Kohler Design Center, where 200,000 people annually come to learn of the history and growth of both the Village and Kohler Co.*

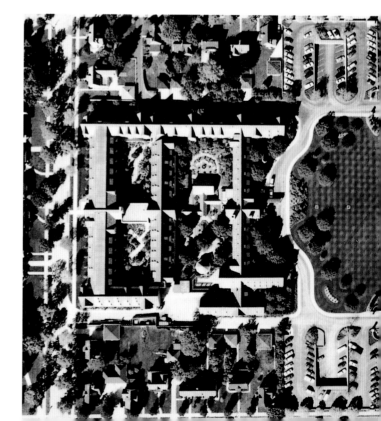

River Wildlife: *The "Second 50-Year Plan" was officially adopted by the Village of Kohler on December 16, 1980. It provided new life for old landscapes and structures—and new landscapes and structures beyond anything previously thought to be possible. River Wildlife is a private wilderness preserve encompassing 500 acres of land, including seven miles of scenic river and 25 miles of trails. The managed preserve combines an abundance of wildlife with year-round sports and outdoor activities.*

Riverbend and Environs: *Another building in need of renewal was Riverbend, the grand estate of former Wisconsin Governor Walter J. Kohler that in 1930 had been acclaimed as one of the 50 most beautiful mansions in America. That history and grandeur of an era long past have been exquisitely restored and given new life as a private club. What could easily have fallen to the wrecking ball, had it not been located within the context of a valued community, has been restored to a level of artistic craftsmanship and attention to detail that appraisers say could not be duplicated today.*

Timeless Land, Timeless Features: *The most durable architecture is inseparable from the natural settings of which it is a feature. Good design radiates an unquestioned sense of belonging. Like the landscape itself, the best design elements are neither new nor old, they are simply part of the fabric of creation.*

237

Creating Heritage: *Selected to host the 2004 PGA Championship, Whistling Straits has won world acclaim since its debut in 1998. It has been artfully sculpted into a two-mile expanse along the Lake Michigan shoreline. The stone clubhouse is shown above. A fortified stone barn, shown on the facing page, opens out to the beauty of the Straits Course and Lake Michigan beyond.*

Earth Art: *In the hands of an artist, a bulldozer is no less a tool than a paintbrush or chisel. All such tools are part of the process in which dreams and feelings are shaped into celebrations of form. The purpose may vary, but not the creative intent. What "White Horse," one of the world's oldest prehistoric carvings, near Uffington in Oxfordshire, England, and the sculptural character of Whistling Straits have in common is that they are both large-scale, human creations. At its best, the ground we shape today need be no less artful than that which we preserve from long ago. It is only by being creative in the here and now that humanity leaves a record worthy of being preserved for generations to come.*

240

Designing the Future

TEN

Complexity and Self-Interest

There is no more futile block to progress than trying to avoid complexity. It is far easier for one nation to overpower another than to work through the checks and balances required to achieve common ground. The command-and-control style is always management's first choice, as long as there is a work force that can be intimidated. The ease of suburbia spread like wildfire until it became the poster child for urban sprawl. That which is easy to understand, easy to build and easy to sell has long been humanity's path of least resistance.

But the easy is rarely the most satisfying. Why else would couples have children? Why would anyone maintain an exercise regimen, build a business or strive to create a work of art? Why do we prepare nutritious meals, read books or study music and dance? Why else would the strong reach out to help the weak? Why would we have teachers, and why would we form religious organizations, country clubs and other groups where the challenging issues of human complexity are ever present? We do so because the rewards are inseparable from the joys of life. Most compelling of all, somewhere in the process, the equation reverses. We either pay the price for what seemed easy or reap the rewards from what seemed difficult.

Nothing looks easier than the seemingly effortless delivery of a master. A beautiful design, an exceptional performance of music or the commanding presence of a great person are all examples of the simplicity that only exists on the other side of complexity. This is the breakthrough into the rewards of a life well designed and well executed, the very same breakthrough that has been the motivation for creating the cultural elements of community since the beginning of time.

The more all people in any one area, nation and eventually the entire earth come in contact with each other, the more essential it becomes to see the creation of community with a sense of what might be termed "urgent joy." Those who seek the rewards of community ask very different questions and play for higher stakes than those who sit on the sidelines wanting it all to be easy. Fortunately, the future is in the hands of those who never stop seeking a better way. Strengths and advantages accrue to those who see life as a performance that demands unending practice in order to give whatever best we each have to offer.

Beyond the Obvious

The body of any great ship will always be far larger and more in evidence than its comparatively tiny rudder, but it is this unseen device from which the ship takes its direction. It isn't the highest volume developers who are creating the future. More often than not, they are locked into an assembly line over which they exercise little or no control. It isn't so much that they know how things must be done; rather, for them, it is the only way they can operate. They are prisoners of their own knowing. Like the rudder on a great ship, if and when they change direction, it will be because they have received a signal from an unseen source that they may have believed to be far behind them. Because we are all in this together, neither the rudder (the special case) nor the ship (volume production) can be at its best without the contribution of the other.

The greatest variable in our future success will be determined by how willing we are to explore beyond the obvious of today, and how quickly we are able to take advantage of what we learn. Even more important is shedding all preconceived ideas about how we think things need to work in order to make sense. In this regard, the whole world of market studies and focus groups will be seen as an outdated block to progress. Anything that can't be seen through the analysts' selected windshields doesn't exist, which allows them to speak with an authority that no creative voice could ever match. The only problem is that what they mistake for windshields are all rearview mirrors.

To understand how dramatic this shift in designing the future will be, think in terms of our now orderly and linear approach. We speak of infrastructure as though it were separate from everything else. Then we speak of the building blocks of community. At the heart of our clarity is the ability to draw boundaries around free-standing things that can be leased or sold with no need to consider the totality. This segregation of the pieces is so basic to our thought process that to consider doing otherwise occasions extensive documentation that provides for legal separations to overcome our fear of physical relatedness. The most common examples are the elaborate covenants, conditions and restrictions that are now required to let people live as everyone once lived without giving it any thought.

"Holistic thinkers are more open to inspiration than others because they instinctively ask questions that others do not: What inner components give this thing its form? Of what larger forms is this thing an element? How does participation in these larger forms affect its identity? These questions open up a variety of perspectives, make the mind fertile for new ideas, and equip us to appreciate the apparent discontinuities—the surprising anomalies—that can result in important discoveries."

– Robert Grudin
*The Grace of Great Things:
Creativity and Innovation*

More Than Tourism

Given that tourism has become the world's number-one industry, it is unlikely that many would agree with Ralph Waldo Emerson, who said that, "The first thing one learns about travel is that it is a fool's paradise." He wasn't trying to discourage exploration but was pointing out that the places we admire most didn't get to be great because people went "gadding about like moths around a candle flame," but because someone stayed there and made them great.

There is much about Emerson's observation that relates to what it takes to create artful communities. With very few Grand Canyon-like exceptions, the world's most magnetic tourist attractions are not the works of nature alone but rather the structures and communities in beautiful settings that have been designed, built and occupied by humans. And the cities we enjoy visiting most are those that are working well for those who live there. If this genuine sense of creation and habitation is missing, the result can be nothing but a theme park in which the only life a transient tourist could experience would be the comings and goings of other transient tourists, hardly anything to write home about.

Places like Disneyland and the Las Vegas strip illustrate what tourism becomes when the only citizenry consists of other tourists. When we visit such places, we visit empty shells that have no meaning without our presence, and our presence occurs without commitment. Except for the paid performers, everyone is an observer with nothing to hope for beyond some momentary, risk-free titillation. There is nothing wrong with enjoying places like this, unless we begin to mistake them for the real thing. And for those committed to the idea that the best is always yet to be, there will never be any doubt that to live fully requires more than simply enjoying the achievements of those long gone. Such places should serve as our inspiration to desire, explore, design and build with as much greatness as our own creativity and commitment permits. To do otherwise would be to squander our inheritance. The person who left this graffiti on a wall in Florence, Italy wouldn't have anything to visit and see if everyone took his or her advice.

"They change their climate, not their soul, who rush across the sea."

– Horace

"Too often travel, instead of broadening the mind, merely lengthens the conversation."

– Elizabeth Drew

The Planetary Challenge

Paleontologist and Jesuit priest Teilhard de Chardin once remarked that God made the world round so that one day we would have to confront each other. That day is now. The time is passing when individuals, groups and nations can ignore the totality of which we are all a part. All human pursuits, including education, religion and commerce, as well as concerns about the environment, technology, war and, most recently, terrorism, are making us "confront each other" as never before.

New Problems, New Opportunities

The exponential growth of the earth's population is currently 200,000 persons per day, the equivalent of adding the population of San Francisco every three days or a new Tokyo every six weeks. Every seven days, the earth adds a population equivalent to a new Phoenix, and every eight weeks, the equivalent of the combined states of Arizona, Kansas and Connecticut. Every three years, we are joined by another quarter of a billion people, the same increase that, in the 18th century, took 75 years, or 25 times as long.

From Neighborhoods to the World

While we may not see ourselves as being able to address the entire planet, we are daily participants in its creation. Every move we make reflects the world in miniature. We are living at a time that cries out for a balance between military readiness and the need to become more attuned to the long, cool view of nature. The ability for micro-weaponry to inflict crippling atrocities is lessening the power of all weapons to provide for long-term safety.

As the illusion of safety by force declines, the compelling need for safety and well-being by community becomes more critical. This time our quest will be increasingly holistic.

For most of human history, fortunes have been made by those whose power resulted from thinking in short-term, fragmented ways. Examples include various forms of master and slave, economic success at the expense of the biosphere, and the easy production of high-volume sprawl as opposed to the far greater demands of creating comprehensive communities. While humanity has always had philosophers, scientists and others who have seen the world in more holistic terms, such voices have seldom ruled the day. In a territorial sense, the first 20 centuries have been dominated by a frontier mentality that has now run its earthly course. Such exploration will continue into the cosmos, but for Planet Earth, it should be evident to all that it is time for frontier values and fragmented thinking to leave center stage.

Reasons to Live and Hope

Again quoting Teilhard de Chardin, "The future is in the hands of those who can give tomorrow's generations valid reasons to live and hope." And this time, feel-good political rhetoric won't do the trick. The tables are already turning. Future power and fortunes will come to those who can demonstrate an ability to achieve successful relationships—between privacy and community, between cities and towns, between nations and, ultimately, between humanity and the earth.

The Role of Design

To visualize a successful future, we first need to sweep aside all the arbitrary "impossibilities" of conventional wisdom. A good next step would be to apply the lessons learned from large-scale planning to the entire surface of the earth.

1 Assume that global conflicts will continue but with no more or less effect on the underlying land use and circulation patterns than has resulted from all past conflicts.

2 Establish seven categories of open space, including:

- Oceans, lakes and river systems
- Frontier forests
- Wilderness parks
- "Production" land, i.e., farms, ranches, forests and mines
- Urban preserves
- Active parks
- Connective arteries for drainage, vegetation, wildlife and easements for infrastructure, including transportation.

3 Beyond the seven categories of open space, determine a division between public and private ownership, and set aside one half of each of their portions as a more fine-grained open space network to be designed into the built environment.

4 For thinking about the future, all land not identified in the open space categories should be envisioned in its developed state.

5 Centuries from now, the open space categories will remain untouched, and the environmental damage inflicted during the 20th century will have healed. The areas set aside for development will have changed to accommodate the heights and densities of the new and continually redeveloping land uses, transportation systems, and building forms and technology.

6 Issues of governance and economic systems will be considered on a global scale but with as much independence as possible at each successive level. Unwise subsidies that were originally more political in nature will be redirected toward restoration ecology.

7 Public support for conservation will forever memorialize the scientist and Pulitzer Prize winner E.O. Wilson's goal of "Half the world for humanity, half for the rest of life, to create a planet both self-sustaining and pleasant."

"All the inhabitants of the planet could theoretically be linked together for instantaneous communication as closely as the inhabitants of a village."

– Lewis Mumford

"The new electronic interdependence recreates the world in the image of a global village."

– Marshall McLuhan

"It is time to sort out earth and calculate what it will take to provide a satisfying and sustainable life for everyone into the indefinite future."

– Edward O. Wilson

Epilogue

Throughout the writing of this book, I have held in mind two very different kinds of people, both of whom I regard to be critically important to the future but who do not have that same regard for each other. This is unfortunate because they could be of mutual benefit; but it remains a most uneasy fit.

The first is the person who has mastered the ways and means of the present as evidenced by his or her success, measured in terms of the proverbial bottom line. The second is the person whose success can only be measured in how effective he or she has been in researching and advancing a position that has not yet been of interest to the marketplace. I value the first because the future requires a successful present, including relevant, accountable and excellent execution. I value the second because tomorrow's success will demand more than an ever-expanding version of the present.

The difficulty in holding this balance is that, other than in hindsight, humanity has never found an easy way to determine the difference between a visionary upon whom society will one day depend and one who is simply delusional. Buckminster Fuller used to refer to this as the need to distinguish between the red berries in the forest that will kill us as opposed to those that will make us big and strong. Within these two types of people (the relevant and the visionary) are those who possess some characteristics of the other. These are the "bridge builders," and they are the light of the world. My one wish for this book is that it might encourage the bridging instinct in each of us. The world of design, development and governance is awash in a torrent of analysis. If studies, words and pictures could make this a better world, we would all be living in peace and splendor. We are the most analyzed, measured and documented people who have ever lived. We know more about each other on a global scale than has ever been possible in the past. Innovative designs in one part of the world are quickly picked up and reproduced everywhere else. Officials, designers, developers and builders are in constant communication, sharing stories of their successes, as well as mistakes made and lessons learned. If one chose to do so, life could be lived in one unending seminar on how to design and develop community.

The limitations of such learning became brutally clear to me while watching one of my partners conclude an elaborate and well thought-out presentation. Instead of his presentation being the start of a promising exploration, the developer's marketing consultant responded with a thoughtless remark that killed off any further consideration. "I'm not saying it isn't the right thing to do, I'm just telling you it won't work." The consultant was right; in fact he was always right. How can you be wrong if your audience is willing to accept an accurate description of yesterday as prophecy? As with all progress, in order to generate a new idea, one has to first inoculate the present with a desire for something better. Otherwise, those who know everything about the past will have no capacity to learn anything they don't already know.

Community Is the *"And"*

There is a Sufi saying that goes something like this, "Because we know the value of *one* and because we know the value of *two*, we think we also know the value of *one* and *two*, but we fail to take into account the value of *and*."

Because community is the *and*, it is far more than a collection of our favorite houses and streets. And rather than being able to define it in terms of the biggest or best, it is a quality we are more likely to be able to feel than to describe. How do you describe the value of *and*?

It is the pursuit of the answer to this question that has guided the writing of this book. While its illustrations are those of streets, bridges, vehicles, signage, houses, buildings, lakes and gardens, its purpose—like that of community itself—is more about connections than anything to do with the individual elements. Community is the spirit of human intention that brings all such elements into overlapping patterns of relationships. It is these relationships, both natural and constructed, that create what we ultimately value most.

The power of relatedness and the authenticity of places that evolve from purpose are made beautifully clear in the following paragraph, quoted from the Chautauqua Institution's "Statement of Philosophy:"

"No single building at Chautauqua is, perhaps, of the first importance architecturally. However, in the aggregate they form a uniquely important collection. Removing any one may weaken the texture of the whole. The collection of buildings at the Chautauqua Institution represents in concrete, visible form many of the historical forces that culminated in the Chautauqua movement and that were central to American history as a whole."

The wide-ranging examples described in these 10 chapters have only one thing in common. None could have existed without the work and commitment of specific individuals who harbored dreams far beyond what precedent or formulas could ever consider or achieve. May their examples inspire us to reach beyond reason into the realm where our very presence may be the key to making good things happen.

"Again and again someone in the crowd wakes up,
he has no ground in the crowd,
And he emerges according to much broader laws.
He carries strange customs with him
and demands room for bold gestures.
The future speaks ruthlessly through him."

– Rainer Maria Rilke

Voices for the Future of Community

"If you go back into the history of humankind, you find that in all the great cultures—the Greek, the Babylonian, the Chinese, the Japanese, and our own—everything begins with a dream."

– Laurens van der Post

"The quantum mechanical view of reality startles us out of common notions of what is real... In the quantum world, relationship is the key determiner of everything... There are no basic building blocks... unseen connections between what were previously thought to be separate entities are the fundamental ingredient of all creation."

– Margaret J. Wheatley

"The fact is that we live in a designed world and will never live in any other kind. Even if nostalgia were functional, and we could return to the simpler life we long for and claim to remember, we would have to design it. Equestrian hauling, wind-powered mills, compost-centered communes are now designed ventures, where once they were invented responses to immediate needs."

– Ralph Caplan

"You are here in order to enable the world to live more amply, with greater vision, with a finer spirit of hope and achievement. You are here to enrich the world, and you impoverish yourself if you forget the errand."

– Woodrow Wilson

"A new degree of culture would instantaneously revolutionize the entire system of human pursuits."

– Ralph Waldo Emerson

"All progress depends on the unreasonable man."
– George Bernard Shaw

"The long view is the cool view. Tolerance, experiment and change give a culture strength. Life always rides in strength to victory, not through (any movement), any 'ism,' but through individual responsibility and initiative."
– Frank Lloyd Wright

"By community I mean, rather, places in which the bonds between people and those between people and the natural world create a pattern of connectedness, responsibility and mutual need. Real communities foster dignity, competence, participation and opportunities for good work. And good communities provide places in which children's imagination and earthly sensibilities root and grow."
– David W. Orr

"I hold that man is in the right who is most closely in league with the future."
– Henrik Ibsen

"Most events are inexpressible, taking place in a realm which no word has ever entered, and more inexpressible than all else are works of art, mysterious existences, the life of which, while ours passes away, endures."
– Rainer Maria Rilke

"When we build, let us think that we will build forever."
– John Ruskin

Definitions

While the language of this book endeavors to be sufficiently balanced to speak for all of us, it is nevertheless a crusading document that reflects the editorial values of the author, who presents the following definitions to reinforce the advocacy of the text.

Architecture and Planning The art and science of bridging between the past and the future, the timeliness of technology and the timelessness of humanity. It is a link between the beauty of nature and the needs of urban living. It is the connective tissue between individual structures and the community as a whole.

Automobile The most effective form of personal transit ever invented, because it is the only one capable of transporting people and things from any place to any other place, at any time. In the near future, we will see greater emphasis on the design and utilization of cars to reduce congestion. By thinking and planning comprehensively, passenger miles, number of vehicles, fuel consumption and pollution per capita will diminish, while mobility (and more importantly) accessibility will increase. It isn't the automobile that gets in the way of community, it is that we have been unwilling to be more artful in thinking about integrated land uses.

Beauty Physicists speak of the "beauty principle" or "coherency theory." When faced with a range of postulates, if one is more beautiful, coherent and elegant, it is pursued as the more plausible of the group. In community development, the search for beauty is far more than simple opinion. It is the search for fundamental principles that will stand the test of time.

Bits and Atoms The miniaturizing made possible by the electronic revolution. "Atoms" refer to moving the mass of objects like cars and packaging. "Bits" move information invisibly, weightlessly and at the speed of light.

Broadacre City Frank Lloyd Wright's concept for decentralization. Unlike today's even spread of suburbia, Broadacre City would have placed more than half of all dwellings in higher-density clusters, with the rest on one acre or more. His concept was characterized by abundant open space and community features.

Cause and Effect What exists today did not just happen. It is the cumulative result of daily decisions both large and small.

Change Something we all tend to resist, but in vain. The Greek philosopher Heraclitus said it long ago, "The only immutable law is the law of change."

Character	Artful relationships designed to create interest, identity and value beyond what would be possible without an overall philosophy and long-term guidance.
Citizen Commitment	A dedication to the values and strategies that can be demonstrated to have long-term benefits for the community.
Citizen Outrage	Usually motivated by something personal. May or may not be informed. Sometimes helpful, sometimes destructive.
Citizen Visioning	Must be inclusive of all interests. Directed to the future but rich in memory. Requires that the participants be extensively informed and willing to embark on a shared exploration with neither preconceived ideas nor personal agendas.
City Building	Humanity's most demanding task. It is the physical synthesis of all that we are and do, embracing everything from the creative to the remedial.
Clustered Development	Higher-density structures arranged in proximity to create resultant open space. It is not simply higher density. In fact, clustering may or may not represent a change in the overall density.
Codes and Ordinances	We have created many negative, "Thou shalt not" injunctions in response to past abuse. To be effective, all codes should be subject to periodic review. When they get in the way of good solutions, codes should be revised or eliminated.
Cohousing	A cluster of private residences, usually with shared facilities that may include a combined kitchen and dining area, shops, meeting rooms, educational or entertainment facilities, and gardens. A critical distinction is that the initial residents take part in shaping the layout and structures of community.
Community	Old definition: multi-generational, centralized development necessitated by limited opportunity, limited mobility and limited means of non-local communication. New definition: dynamic and decentralized development based on opportunity, mobility and unprecedented technology for global communication.
Complexity and Integration	Nature's basic lesson. The interdependence that underlies the workings of all natural systems is ultimately necessary for the design of successful human settlements.
Connective Tissue	The conscious understanding and use of open space that is coordinated with street trees, walls, fences, signage, lighting and other devices designed to create an overall community fabric.

Decentralization A force so pervasive it underlies everything from the architecture of communities to the architecture of the Internet. It is the emerging polycentric city pattern that is steadily replacing the single core ringed with suburbs.

Decentralized Success What *Edge City* author Joel Garreau calls that "squishy stuff... There has to be civilization, soul, identity. Is this going to be a good place for me to grow old? For my kids to grow up? Could you imagine having a Fourth of July parade here?"

Density The number of residential units per acre. Too often misused as a measure of quality, i.e., in the false belief that lower densities are better than higher densities. This is often a meaningless measure in itself. When density becomes the most compelling issue in land-use decisions, it tends to discredit all other considerations. Density has meaning only when expressed for a specific purpose and context. There are good examples of 100 acres per unit as well as 100 units per acre. To be "for" or "against" density, in the abstract, is meaningless.

Design and Exploration Both require the acceptance of limits as well as extensive preparation for the journey. The dialogue of design and exploration is most effective if accompanied by an understanding of the alternatives.

Developer This is a value-laden word, like "sprawl." It should have no implied meaning. There are enlightened developers and abusive ones.

Edge City From Joel Garreau's best-selling book, *Edge City, Life on the New Frontier*, in which he describes the emergence of large concentrations of urban activity that has happened outside our more planned areas.

Electronic Revolution The capacity to make invisible certain aspects of the information, communication and transportation processes within the urban environment. The ability to deliver more services at less cost.

Environmentalist Old definition: any form of "tree hugger" who tries to protect the "natural" world from human use. New definition: anyone who accepts humanity as basic to nature and works to create more beautiful and sustainable relationships between the two.

Future In the words of futurist Arthur Clarke, "The future is always unknown and unknowable." In terms of planning, the future is a consequence selected from a range of possible options.

Garage   The most difficult element to absorb in moderate-density housing. There are eight known possibilities:

- Front- and/or side-loaded, garage-dominated streets
- Garage-free streets, with garage-dominated alleys
- The old Charleston arrangement, which has front-access, narrow lanes capable of parking three cars in single file in the side yard with no garage
- Eight-foot-wide front lanes to garages located in the rear of the lot
- Same as above but with shared driveways to further enhance the street scene
- A single access to a central courtyard of garages
- Underground or on-grade clustered garage spaces separate from each house
- Mobility centers of readily available shared vehicles, permitting the reduction or elimination of car storage at individual residences

General Plan   Also known as the Comprehensive Plan. An always time-bound instrument subject to periodic updates and changes. In a largely empty landscape, like the desert Southwest, if the general plan changes without due deliberation, it is an irresponsible document. If it never changes, it is either divinely inspired or blindly unresponsive to the evolving needs of the community.

Green Design   The name given to methods, systems and materials that seek to conserve land, energy and water, including all methods for the re-use of materials that would otherwise be discarded or used in a wasteful manner.

Heroic Structures   Buildings that give extraordinary identity to an area but that today might be disallowed as too aggressive for their sensitive settings. Historic examples include Thomas Jefferson's Lawn at the University of Virginia, Frederick Law Olmsted's Central Park, Frank Lloyd Wright's Fallingwater, King Ludwig II's Neuschwanstein Castle, and urban settlements such as Machu Picchu, Chichén Itzá, the Alhambra or the hill towns of Italy and France. Examples from the American Southwest include Mesa Verde, Chaco Canyon, Walpi and Taliesin West. In addition to their historic value, these examples serve as inspiration for each generation to build something of significance for the future.

Indigenous Architecture   Design that evolves out of the land's heritage, climate and character and does not depend on preconceived styles. Like the mountains, indigenous design is more timeless than that which goes in and out of fashion.

Individuality and Community Related but not the same. Individuality may opt for larger lots, private open space and freedom from interference. Community is interdependent and interactive. Individuality and community are not mutually exclusive. We all have the need for both.

Infill Development The use of skipped-over or abandoned sites, generally in proximity to older, more urban portions of the community.

Integrity Anything true to itself, including the honest use of materials, architectural designs and landscapes that complement their settings.

Light-Rail Transit A modern form of streetcar that is experiencing a resurgence in popularity as a partial solution to the problem of urban mobility.

Live/Work Any pattern of relationships that permits a pedestrian connection between one's home and place of business, thus eliminating the back-and-forth commute.

Luxury Most of the old luxuries remain, but where development is concerned, the new luxuries include:

- A home experience that extends beyond the house

- Privacy and individuality with community

- Less hassle miles, more accessibility

- Innovative settings for live/work

- Anything "custom"

Man/Nature Balance Dan Kiley, one of this country's most distinguished and honored landscape architects, suggests that, "Man and his environment are inseparable, that it's not man and nature or man in nature but man as nature, just like the trees."

Market Forces "Laws" of expected seller/buyer response. Unlike the laws of gravity, market forces are created by human activities and are thus subject to manipulation and change.

Mixed-Use A complexity of functions allowing for all manner of community provisions, including work, home, shopping, schools, restaurants, entertainment, parks, and civic buildings all within close proximity.

Moratorium A costly substitute for vision. At best, it provides time for the community to catch its breath. At worst, it transfers any hope for quality to the lose/lose game of litigation. When we call "time out," we should know it is impossible to win the game without putting the ball back in play.

Neighborhood A physical setting with perceivable edges and characteristics that can be felt upon entering and leaving. It is the shared setting of which each structure is a feature. It is the transitional space between one's home and the broader community.

Neotraditional Planning Also called "new urbanism" or Traditional Neighborhood Development (TND). A return to the pedestrian-friendly, more integrated land-use patterns of the 1920s, characterized by streets arranged on an open, mainly rectangular grid, with alleys and traditionally styled houses on smaller lots.

No Growth A meaningless phrase because it doesn't exist. Communities either grow or die. The notion of "no growth" provides a good example of the polarizing misuse of words. Rather than facing the difficulty of exploration and design, it makes it possible to simply choose sides.

Opposition and Argument While they can be enlightening activities, neither requires ownership or preparation. In the arena of public debate, opposition or argument allows one to enter the dialogue without risk or in-depth knowledge of the subject.

Pattern Language From a book by the architect Christopher Alexander, in which he discusses how what we build affects us in the long run. The underlying assumption is that there is something observable to be considered that exists beyond mere opinion or taste.

Pessimism/Optimism Two views of the future, both needed. Pessimism reminds us to scrutinize our doubts so that our preparation will be thorough. Optimism reminds us to value our dreams so that our thoroughness will be sufficiently worthwhile.

Planning Too often a long drawn-out process of answering questions necessary to comply with codes, ordinances, market studies, financing and the imperatives of production. Good planning requires going beyond the obvious to address questions that are not likely to be asked.

Porch An addition to production housing of which the following reasons (a) and (b) are true, while (c) is more seeming than real: (a) Front porches add the interest of articulated shade and shadow to otherwise boxy structures; (b) Porches are friendly for reasons of nostalgia, and because they imply that someone could sit there; (c) People sit on their porches, converse with their neighbors and provide a friendly sense of surveillance over the neighborhood.

Possible/Impossible Not so much statements of inevitable truth as judgments based on whatever assumptions seem to govern decision-making in a given place and time. When what works is "impossible" and what is "possible" doesn't work, it is time to widen the exploration.

Public Transit A once dominant form of urban transportation. At the end of World War II, transit accounted for 35 percent of all urban travel, as opposed to five percent today. To understand the consequences of lifestyle and density, for every mile the Japanese ride on fixed rail transportation, they drive two miles on the road. In the United States, for every mile we ride on fixed rail transportation, we drive 288 miles of the road. To design for its most effective use, we need to be more accurate and honest about what public transit can and cannot do.

Regional Open Space Because it needs to be vast and as contiguous as possible, the definition should include all non-building areas, including parks, golf courses, path systems, scenic easement, transit corridors, selected mining, ranching and agricultural areas, drainageways, mountaintops, upper slopes, riparian habitats, special reserves such as military bases, and last but not least, ecological preserves with little or no routine access. All nonbuilding areas are open space, whether in private or public ownership.

Relevant/Irrelevant To speak with relevance is to risk lacking vision. To speak with vision is to risk appearing irrelevant. What society needs most is to build bridges between the obvious of today and the unseen but achievable realities of tomorrow.

Rezoning All zoning is a rezoning. It is an imposed limitation applied to specific pieces of land at specific points in time, based on whatever information seems compelling to both the concerned citizens and public officials having jurisdiction over the land. In a growing, changing community, land-use restrictions are either justified by their evolving context or they become candidates for reconsideration. When this occurs, change must be approved by the same procedures and safeguards that created the prior zoning.

Rural Development Characterized by informal patterns of development with a low gross density. The area may include clustered pockets of higher densities.

Sense of Community When we speak of designing master-planned communities, the phrase combines that which can be constructed with that which must be allowed to emerge over time. A community does not happen until people interact and make the setting their own. The best plans are not those that are easily measurable in "things." Rather, they are the framework for garden-like settings and interrelationships that are rich in human values and the potential to nurture growth.

Scientific Facts	Always good to pursue, but the creation of community is far more dependent on human values than on scientific facts. Whether or not we are building wisely goes well beyond the reach of easy measures.
Soul	Beyond codes and ordinances, beyond bits and atoms, beyond short-term profit and loss, there exists a quality on which all else depends. See the Charles Kuralt quote regarding neighborhoods at the beginning of Chapter Eight.
Street Scene	What one sees and feels along the edges and pathways of the city. It is shaped by adjacent buildings and articulated by landscaping and lighting, as well as by the color and texture of paving and signage. The street scene should be thought of as a community space to be designed with great care.
Sustainable Community	Sustainability is not a matter of technology nor is it a single-issue idea. It is an attitude which views the interaction of whole systems. Judgments as to what works and what does not must now include the variables of land use, circulation, infrastructure, building systems and patterns of human behavior. Any thought that there is a code-like formula for sustainable development is a bureaucratic illusion.
Telecommuting	Eliminates distance as a factor. Certain physical trips need not occur. Unlike most means of travel, telecommuting knows no limits. It changes the ground rules of proximity. It is no longer necessary to cross town in order to meet face to face. Businesses located in one country can have their word processing done in another. Some have called this "the death of distance."
Thoughtless Development	The kind of mindless production that erupts most often when the economy is hot. This thoughtlessness is not only bad for the environment, it is bad for the economy, in that it inspires opposition to *all* development.
Three-Dimensional Planning	Configuring land-use studies with full awareness of the topography and the intended character of the built environment. Every planning opportunity comes with a set of abilities and expectations that either empowers or limits the process. It is all far more than the making of two-dimensional maps.

Timely and Timeless   Cyberspace is timely and subject to rapid, ongoing change. It knows no boundaries. It creates "neighborhoods" that are not defined by physical shape and adjacency. In contrast, the beauty of nature and the human need for space and artful environments are timeless. Everything is subject to change, but technology and geology do not change at the same rate. Timely and timeless are not in conflict. We need to recognize their differences in order to design for each accordingly.

TODs   Transit Oriented Development in which higher-density, mixed-use planning is clustered around existing or planned transit stops.

Traditional   A loosely defined but currently dominant appearance of production housing. Nearly every recent builder competition has produced winners that look as though they were designed in the 1920s. Doesn't it at least make you wonder what all those little boys and girls who dreamt of becoming creative architects are doing?

Urban Development   As opposed to rural development. Characterized by a more self-conscious, imposed pattern of relationships between structures, streets and open space.

Urban Limit Lines   Also known as Urban Growth Boundaries. A government-imposed line that divides land that can be developed as part of the metropolitan expansion and that which must remain rural—at least until such time that the line may be moved to accommodate more growth.

Urban Sprawl   The too-even distribution of look-alike, homogenous uses lacking in recognizable form or character. An endless sameness, unrelieved by significant structures or open space. An awkward spread of development without discernible edges.

Utopia or Oblivion   Buckminster Fuller prophesied that these extremes would one day become our only two choices. We can either go full-speed ahead toward creating optimal communities or, failing to do so, we can engage in ever-increasing confrontation in which everybody loses.

Variance for Excellence   Provisions for allowing special land uses and creative designs to occur that do not necessarily meet existing codes or ordinances, but represent a demonstrably better way.

Vision   It all begins with an optimistic spirit. Beyond the expedient is a future that will stand the test of time. It is our vision for an ideal world that will give us guidance for the real world. The most effective visions are in alignment with long-term market forces.

Selected References

Aldous, Tony. *Urban Villages*. London: The Urban Villages Group, 1992.

Alexander, Christopher, Sara Ishikawa and Murray Silverstein. *A Pattern Language: Towns, Buildings, Construction*. New York: Oxford University Press, 1977.

Arendt, Randall and Holly Harper. *Conservation Design for Subdivisions: A Practical Guide to Creating Open Space Networks*. Washington, D.C.: Island Press, 1996.

Bellah, Robert N., Richard Madsen, William M. Sullivan, Ann Swidler and Steven M. Tipton. *The Good Society*. New York: Vintage Books, 1991.

——. *Habits of the Heart, Individualism and Commitment in American Life*. Berkeley: Perennial Library, Harper & Row, 1985.

Belto, David T., Peter Gordon and Alexander Tabarrok. *The Volunteer City: Choice, Community and Civic Society*. Ann Arbor, Michigan: The University of Michigan Press, 2002.

Benfield F. Kaid, Jutka Terris and Nancy Vorsanger. *Solving Sprawl, Models of Smart Growth in Communities Across America*, New York, NY: Natural Resources Defense Council, 2001.

Bernick, Michael and Robert Cervero. *Transit-Based Residential Development in the United States: A Review of Recent Experiences*. Berkeley: University of California at Berkeley, Institute of Urban and Regional Development, 1994.

Beveridge, Charles E. and Paul Rocheleau. *Frederick Law Olmsted: Designing the American Landscape*. New York: Rizzoli International Publications, Inc., 1995.

Bookout, Lloyd W. *Value by Design: Landscape, Site Planning and Amenities*. Washington, D.C.: The Urban Land Institute, 1994.

BPI Communications. *Architecture–Rebuilding America's Cities*. New York: Volume 84, Number 4, August, 1995.

Braungart, Michael and William Mc Donough. *Cradle to Cradle: Remaking the Way We Make Things*. New York, New York: North Point Press, 2002.

Calthorpe, Peter. *The Next American Metropolis: Ecology, Community and the American Dream*. New York: Princeton Architectural Press, 1993.

—— and William Fulton. *The Regional City*. Washington, D.C.: Island Press, 2001.

Cervero, Robert. *The All-Electric Commute: An Assessment of the Market Potential for Station Cars in the San Francisco Bay Area*. Berkeley: University of California at Berkeley, Institute of Urban and Regional Development, 1994.

—— and Michael Bernick. *Transportation Alternatives in a Congestion Pricing Environment*. Berkeley: University of California at Berkeley, Institute of Urban and Regional Development, 1992.

Dagget, Dan. *Beyond the Rangeland Conflict: Toward a West That Works*. Layton, Utah: Gibbs Smith and the Grand Canyon Trust, 1995.

Davis, Stan and Bill Davidson. *2020 Vision.* New York: Simon & Schuster, 1991.

Day, Christopher. *Places of the Soul: Architecture and Environmental Design as a Healing Art.* Northamptonshire, England: The Aquarian Press, 1990.

Downs, Anthony. *Stuck in Traffic, Coping With Peak-Hour Traffic Congestion.* Washington, D.C.: The Brookings Institution and The Lincoln Institute of Land Policy, Cambridge, Massachusetts, 1992.

Dyson, Freeman. *Infinite in All Directions.* New York: Harper and Row, 1988.

Eaton, Ruth. *Ideal Cities: Utopianism and the (Un)Built Environment.* New York, New York: Thames & Hudson, Ltd., 2001.

Ehrenhalt, Alan. *The Lost City.* New York: Basic Books, Inc., 1995.

Ekins, Paul. *The Gaia Atlas of Green Economics.* New York: Anchor Books, Doubleday, 1992.

Findlay, John M. *Magic Lands: Western Cityscapes and American Culture After 1940.* Berkeley: University of California Press, 1992.

Fishman, Robert. *Urban Utopias in the Twentieth Century.* New York: Basic Books, Inc., 1977.

Fleming, Ronald Lee. *Façade Stories: Changing Faces of Main Street Storefronts and How to Care for Them.* New York: Hastings House Publishers, 1982.

——. *Saving Face: How Corporate Franchise Design Can Respect Community Identity.* Chicago: The American Planning Association, 1994.

Fleming, Ronald Lee and Lauri A. Halderman. *On Common Ground: Caring for Shared Land From Town Common to Urban Park.* Cambridge: Harvard Common Press, 1982.

Fuller, R. Buckminster. *Utopia or Oblivion.* Santa Barbara: Buckminster Fuller Institute, 1969.

Garreau, Joel. *Edge City: Life on the New Frontier.* New York: Double Day, 1988.

Girling, Cynthia L. and Kenneth I. Helphand. *Yard, Street, Park: The Design of Suburban Open Space.* New York: John Wiley & Sons, Inc., 1994.

Goldsteen, Joel B. and Cecil D. Elliott. *Designing America: Creating Urban Identity.* New York: Van Nostrand Reinhold, 1994.

Goodman, Paul and Percival Goodman. *Communitas: Means of Livelihood and Ways of Life.* New York: Vintage Books, 1947.

Gratz, Roberta Brandes. *The Living City: How America's Cities Are Being Revitalized by Thinking Small in a Big Way.* Washington, D.C.: The Preservation Press, 1989.

Grudin, Robert. *The Grace of Great Things: Creativity and Innovation.* New York: Ticknor & Fields, 1990.

Hale, Jonathan. *The Old Way of Seeing: How Architecture Lost Its Magic (and How to Get It Back).* New York: Houghton Mifflin Co., 1994.

Hawken, Paul. *The Ecology of Commerce: A Declaration of Sustainability.* New York: Harper Business, 1993.

Hirschberg, Jerry. *The Creative Priority, Driving Innovative Business in the Real World,* New York, New York: Harper Collins, 1998.

Howard, Ebenezer. *Garden Cities of To-Morrow.* Cambridge: The M.I.T. Press, 1965.

Howard, Philip K. *The Death of Common Sense: How Law is Suffocating America.* New York: Random House, 1994.

Institute of Transportation Studies. *Restructuring the Automobile/Highway System for Lean Vehicles.* Berkeley: University of California, 1991.

Jacobs, Jane. *The Death and Life of Great American Cities.* New York: Vintage Books, 1992.

Jarvis, Frederick D. *Site Planning and Community Design for Great Neighborhoods.* Washington, D.C.: Home Builder Press, 1993.

Johnson, Steven. *Emergence.* New York: Scribner, 2001.

Katz, Peter. *The New Urbanism: Toward an Architecture of Community.* New York: McGraw-Hill, Inc., 1994.

Kay, Jane Holtz. *Asphalt Nation: How the Automobile Took Over America and How We Can Take It Back.* New York: Crown Publishers, Inc., 1997.

Kemmis, Daniel. *The Good City and the Good Life: Renewing the Sense of Community.* New York: Houghton Mifflin Company, 1995.

Kostof, Spiro. *The City Shaped: Urban Patterns and Meanings Through History.* Toronto, Canada: Bulfinch Press, 1991.

——. *America by Design.* New York: Oxford University Press, 1987.

Kotkin, Joel. *The New Geography: How the Digital Revolution Is Reshaping the American Landscape.* New York: Random House, Inc. 2000.

Krier, Leon. *Houses, Palaces, Cities: Architectural Design Profile.* London: Architectural Design, 1984.

Kunstler, James Howard. *The Geography of Nowhere.* New York: Simon & Schuster, 1993.

——. *Home From Nowhere: Remaking Our Everyday World for the 21st Century.* New York: Simon & Schuster, 1996.

Langdon, Philip. *A Better Place to Live: Reshaping the American Suburb.* Amherst, Massachusetts: The University of Massachusetts Press, 1994.

Larsen, Knud and Armund Sinding-Larsen. *The Lhasa Atlas, Traditional Tibetan Architecture and Townscape.* Boston, Massachusetts: Shambhala, 2001.

Lekson, Stephen H. and Rina Swentzell. *Ancient Land, Ancestral Places: Paul Logsdon in the Pueblo Southwest.* Santa Fe, New Mexico: Museum of New Mexico Press, 1993.

Leopold, Aldo. *A Sand County Almanac.* New York: Oxford University Press, 1977.

Lyle, John Tillman. *Regenerative Design for Sustainable Development.* New York: John Wiley & Sons, Inc., 1994.

McCamant, Kathryn and Charles Durrett. *Cohousing: A Contemporary Approach to Housing Ourselves.* Berkeley: Ten Speed Press, 1988.

McHarg, Ian. *Design With Nature.* Garden City, New York: Natural History Press, 1969.

——. *A Quest for Life.* New York: John Wiley & Sons, 1996.

Moe, Richard and Carter Wilkie. *Changing Places: Rebuilding Community in the Age of Sprawl.* New York: Henry Holt & Co., 1997.

Moore, Charles, Gerald Allen, and Donlyn Lyndon. *The Place of Houses.* New York: Holt, Rinehart and Winston, 1974.

Moore, Charles W. *You Have to Pay for the Public Life.* London, England: Massachusetts Institute of Technology, 2001.

Mumford, Lewis. *The City in History: Its Origin, Its Transformations, and Its Prospects.* New York: Harcourt, Brace & World, 1961.

National Geographic Society. *The Builders: Marvels of Engineering.* Washington, D.C.: National Geographic Society, 1992.

Nelessen, Anton Clarence. *Visions for a New American Dream.* Chicago: American Planning Association, 1994.

Newman, Peter and Jeffrey Kenworthy. *Sustainability and Cities: Overcoming Automobile Dependence.* Washington, D.C.: Island Press, 1999.

Norwood, Ken and Kathleen Smith. *Rebuilding Community in America: Housing for Ecological Living, Personal Empowerment, and the New Extended Family.* Berkeley: Shared Living Resource Center, 1995.

Oldenburg, Ray. *The Great Good Place.* New York: Paragon House, 1991.

Open Spaces, City Places: Contemporary Writers on the Changing Southwest. Tucson, London: The University of Arizona Press, 1994.

Pearson, David. *Earth to Spirit: In Search of Natural Architecture.* San Francisco: Chronicle Books, 1994.

——. *The Natural House Book.* New York: Simon & Schuster, Inc., 1989.

Riley, Robert Q. *Alternative Cars in the 21st Century: A New Personal Transportation Paradigm.* Warrendale, Pennsylvania: Society of Automotive Engineers, Inc., and New York, New York: Random House, 1992.

Rowe, Peter G. *Making a Middle Landscape.* Cambridge: The M.I.T. Press, 1991.

Rudofsky, Bernard. *Architecture Without Architects.* Albuquerque: University of New Mexico Press, 1964.

Rybczynski, Witold. *City Life: Urban Expectations in a New World.* New York: Scribner, 1995.

Safdie, Moshe with Wendy Kohn. *The City After the Automobile: An Architect's Vision.* New York: Basic Books, Inc., 1997.

Schwartz, Peter. *The Art of the Long View.* New York: Doubleday Currency, 1991.

Simonds, John Ormsbee. *Garden Cities 21: Creating a Livable Urban Environment.* New York: McGraw-Hill, Inc., 1994.

Soleri, Paolo. *Arcosanti, An Urban Laboratory?* Mayer, Arizona: The Cosanti Press, 1993.

Stone, Christopher D. *The Gnat Is Older Than Man: Global Environment and Human Agenda.* Princeton, New Jersey: Princeton University Press, 1993.

Sutro, Suzanne. *Reinventing the Village.* Washington, D.C.: American Planning Association, 1990.

Swaback, Vernon D. *Designing the Future.* The Herberger Center for Design Excellence College of Architecture and Environmental Design, Arizona State University: Tempe, Arizona, 1997.

———. *The Custom Home: Dreams, Desire, Design.* The Images Publishing Group Pty. Ltd., Australia, 2001.

Trefil, James S. *A Scientist in the City.* New York: Doubleday, 1994.

Vale, Brenda and Robert Vale. *Green Architecture: Design for an Energy-Conscious Future.* London: Bulfinch Press, 1991.

Wentling, James. *Designing a Place Called Home: Reordering the Suburbs.* New York: Chapman and Hall, 1995.

Wheatley, Margaret J. *Leadership and the New Science: Learning about Organization From an Orderly Universe.* San Francisco: Barrett-Koehler, 1994.

Whyte, William H. *City: Rediscovering the Center.* New York: Doubleday, 1988.

———. *The Last Landscape.* Garden City: Anchor Books, 1970.

Wilson, Edward O. *The Future of Life.* New York: Alfred A. Knopf, 2002.

Wright, Frank Lloyd. *The Living City.* New York: Horizon Press, 1958.

Wright, Robert. *Non-Zero, The Logic of Human Destiny.* New York: Pantheon Books, 2000.

Zygas, K. Paul (Editor). *Frank Lloyd Wright: The Phoenix Papers. Volume 1: Broadacre City.* Tempe: Herberger Center for Design Excellence, 1995.

Credits

Design

Bakken Cohousing: 64 top center

Barry Berkus: 229 top

Stephen Blatt: 79 upper right

Bowden Design Group (Landscaping): 212 to 223

Circle West: 209, 220

Cooper, Robertson: 96, 97

Duany Plater-Zyberk and Dover Kohl: 103 to 105

Santiago Calatrava: 164

Pete Dye: 231 middle & bottom, 238 top, 240, 241

Elliott & Elliott: 120

Barnaby Evans: 161, 162, 163

Foit-Albert: 88

Foster and Partners: 47 bottom

Hayes Architecture/Interiors: 99 top

Housecraft Builders: 67

Goldstone & Heinz: 134 bottom

Kohler Co.: 231 top, 234, 238, 239

Samuel Mockbee: 70 to 73

Claude Monet: 8, 9, 20, 54, 76, 106, 128, 168, 190, 208, 224, 242

Henry Moore: 3

John Morris: 118, 119

Frederick Law Olmsted: 110, 111, 137 bottom, 270, 271

Richard Phillipp/Kohler Co.: 232, 233, 236, 237

Antoine Predock: 68, 69

Paolo Soleri: 60

Sasaki Associates: 3, 108, 134 bottom, 138 left middle, 139 top right

Seaman-Whiteside: 103, 104, 105

Scholz & Barclay: 80

South Mountain Company: 64, 65 all but top center

Robert A.M. Stern: 96, 97

SWA Group: 134 top, 135

Swaback Partners: end papers, 123, 125, 126, 127, 142, 143, 146 to 148, 149, 166, 167, 212, 213, 228 bottom two, 230 top left

Tod Williams, Billie Tsien: 165

Frank Lloyd Wright: 171, 191, 194, 195, 197, 200 to 207

Zmistowski Associates: 218 top, 221

Drawings

All drawings and photographs © by their respective providers

Saverio de Bello: 156 right

D3 Digital Designs: 145

Peter Dozal: 100, 125, 126, 127, 146 to 149

Azad Nana Keli: 189

Knud Larsen and Amund-Sinding Larsen: 172

South Mountain Company: 66

Swaback Partners: end papers, 100, 123, 125, 126, 127, 142, 143, 146 to 149, 198, 204, 205

Photography

AeroMetric: 227

Arcosanti: 60

Yahn Arthus-Bertrand/Corbis: 38, 39

Randi Baird: 65 middle and bottom

David Ball/Corbis: 178 top

Alex Bickel: 92 top center

Chautauqua Institution: 87 to 94

Corbis: 56, 154 top

Richard Davies: 47 bottom

Dennis Degnan/Corbis: 156 left bottom

DMB: 210 to 223

Barnaby Evans: 161, 162, 163

Derek Fell: 8, 9, 20, 54, 76, 106, 128, 168, 190, 208, 224, 242

Chuck Durrett of The Cohousing Company: 64 top

Foit-Albert: 90 bottom

Dale Gardon: 96, 97 top and bottom

Getty Images: 43 middle and left

Bruce Fox: 87 top, 89 top left, 91 middle right, 94 left middle two and bottom right

Dr. George Gerster/Photo Researchers: 241 to 42 bottom center

Jim Gipe: 114

Jason Hawkes: 28 top left, 29, 43 top and bottom right, 155 top

Hayes Architecture/Interiors: 99 top

Jeremy Homer/Corbis: 174

Dave G. Houser/Corbis: 85 right

Timothy Hursley: 68 to 73, 164

Kevin Ireton, Fine Homebuilding: 65 right

Kohler Co.: Cover, 228 to 241

Landiscor: 50 bottom, 52, 53

Sarah Leen/National Geographic: 32, 33

Knud Larsen: 173

Kylene Lloyd: 95 top right

Lawrence Manning/Corbis: 154 bottom

Alex S. MacLean/Landslides: 27, 34, 35, 36 left

Laura Miller: 67

Michael Moran: 165

Arthur Patrick Mullin: 176

Neilson Library Archives: 110 to 113

Nicole Otallah: 84 bottom, 136 top center, 159

Welden Owen: 28, 36 right, 39, 152, 153

Hugh Palmer from The Most Beautiful Village Series, by James Bentley, Thames & Hudson Inc., N.Y.: 4, 30, 31, 136 left, 137 top right, 150, 151

Al Payne: 51

Presbyterian Homes Evanston, Illinois: 116, 117

Mary Quattlebaum: 102 to 105

Dr. Thomas Quattlebaum: 99, 107

Alex Ramsay: 155 bottom

Melissa Roberts: 92 top right

Paul Rocheleau: 137 bottom, 171, 270, 271

Sasaki Associates: 3, 108, 134 bottom, 138 middle left, 139 top right, 140 left, 144

James Spencer: 166, 167

Ted Spiegel/Corbis: 85 left

Roger and Doris Straus: 199 middle

SWA Group: 134 top, 135

Swaback Partners: 42, 46, 47, 74, 75, 99 middle, 100, 109, 136 middle and bottom, 138, 139, 140 right, 152 left middle, 153 top right, 156 top left, 158, 180 to 183, 245

Todd Photographic Services: 50 top

Dino Tonn: 210 to 11 top center, 215 bottom right, 216 top right, 217 top left

John Trotto: 6, 7, 269

Scott Troyanus/Adstock: 57

Brian Vanden Brink: 18, 19, 79 to 83, 118, 119, 120, 133

Brian Vikander/Corbis: 175

Maureen White: 62, 63

Jim Wildeman: 198 to 199 top

Dr. Andrew Wood: 97 middle

Frank Lloyd Wright Foundation: 194 bottom, 200, 201, 202, 203, 204, 205, 206, 207

The Workplace as Community: *Just a few steps from the urban environment, the studio offices of Swaback Partners opens onto a cascading water garden, including the colors and fragrance of an indigenous environment.*

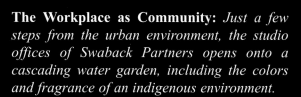

About the Author

Vernon D. Swaback was raised in Chicago, where he first felt the influence of Frank Lloyd Wright. In 1957, he traveled to Arizona to become Wright's youngest apprentice, residing at Taliesin West during the winter months, and during the summers, at Taliesin in Wisconsin. He remained with the Wright organization for 22 years before founding an independent practice. Swaback Partners is now a 40-person firm of architects, planners, landscape architects and interior designers.

Community planning accounts for a third of the firm's involvements. Other commissions are divided equally between the design of custom residences, commercial and institutional buildings. Representative planning work is underway in Utah, California, Hawaii and Mexico. Examples included in this book include the 5,000-acre Village of Kohler, Wisconsin, the 1,000-acre Arizona Biltmore Estates and the 8,300-acre DC Ranch in Scottsdale. Commercial and institutional work includes the Ullman Center at the Phoenix Art Museum, the restoration and expansion of the Arizona Biltmore Hotel, the Scottsdale Water Campus and the largest contemporary rammed-earth structure, designed as the headquarters for a major television station.

Partners of the firm hold architectural registrations in California, Arizona, Colorado, New Mexico, Texas, Missouri, Michigan, Wisconsin, Illinois, Indiana, Kentucky, North Carolina, South Carolina and Florida. Work in other countries has taken them to Russia, Japan, Mexico and Saudi Arabia.

Vernon Swaback's prior writings include *Production Dwellings, An Opportunity for Excellence*, published by the Wisconsin Department of Natural Resources; *Designing the Future*, published by the College of Architecture and Environmental Design at Arizona State University; and *The Custom Home—Dreams, Desire, Design* by Images Publishing of Australia. The author/architect resides with his wife and two daughters in Scottsdale, Arizona.

Vernon Swaback (center) with his partners,
John Sather, AIA, AICP on the left and Jon Bernhard, AIA on the right.

The Poetry of Urban Design: *There will always be a changing supply of codes, ordinances, high-volume production and "bottom lines." Not so inevitable is the commitment and creativity needed to infuse life-sustaining beauty into the rudiments of everyday life. For that, humanity has always counted on those whose special gifts include an ability to see beyond the "wisdom" of the obvious.*

Emerald Necklace Bridge Park System: Boston Park System

"Despite almost universal beliefs to the contrary, gratification, love, comfort, diversion and a state of having achieved all of one's goals do not constitute happiness ... Humans are complex and contradictory beings, egocentric but inescapably involved with their fellow beings, selfish but capable of superb selflessness. We are preoccupied with our own needs, yet find no meaning in life unless we relate ourselves to something more comprehensive than those needs."

– John W. Gardner

"The ultimate test of civilization
is whether or not it contributes to
the improvement of mankind.
Does it uplift, inspire, stimulate
and develop the best in man?
There really can be no other
right purpose to community
except to provide an environment and an opportunity to
develop better people. The most
successful community would be
that which contributed the
most by its physical form, its
institutions and its operations to
the growth of people."

– James W. Rouse